CRUCIFIXION OF CHRIST BY PRESIDENT OBAMA

Elijah Paul

Elijah Paul Ministry

Copyright © 2025 Elijah Paul Ministry

All rights reserved

No part of this book may be reproduced, or stored in a retrieval system, or transmitted in any form or by any means, electronic, mechanical, photocopying, recording, or otherwise, without express written permission of the publisher.

ISBN-13: 9798987467596

Cover design by: Art Painter
Library of Congress Control Number: 2018675309
Printed in the United States of America

CONTENTS

Title Page
Copyright
Church People Will Be Judged First by God on Judgment Day 1
Adding to & Taking from God's Word Causes Sickness & Death 4
Hypocrite Preachers & Some Politicians Are the Worse People on Earth 5
God Heals the Land When Christians Live Holy & Sanctified 7
Friends of the World are Enemies of God 10
God is Always Right but Humans Are Often Wrong 12
We Do & Support Whatever is in Our Heart 14
God Chastises Who He Loves but Rebellious People are Punished Hard 15
All God's Creations Do What He Made Them to Do Except Most Humans 16
We Must Love & Fear God and Not Simply Love Him 19
The Holy Prophets & Apostles Were Greater Than President Obama 22
Martin Luther of Europe & Dr. Martin Luther King, Jr. Were Greater Than President Obama 25
People Shall be Uprooted Who Do Not Produce Godly Deeds 27
If We Expect God to Bless America, We Must Bless & Obey 29

God

Sometimes God Does Not Hear Sinners' Prayers — 31

Obama Nation Became Abomination — 35

Persecution for Standing with God Against Homosexuality — 38

Homophobia & Abomination — 41

Supporting Homosexuality is to Hate & Reject God — 43

God's Judgment on Hypocrite Christians & Nonbelievers — 45

We Must Be Like God to Please God but God is Not Gay — 47

Gays Adopting Children is to Train Children in an Ungodly Way — 48

The Tribes of Ancient Israel Fought a War Against Homosexuality — 50

Nations Are Punished Terribly by God for Homosexuality — 52

Bible Strict & Specific Scriptures Against Homosexuality — 55

The Price of Sin is Death but Punishment Still Happens Before Death — 58

Refusing to Believe that Rebellious People Reap Death, Destruction, & Hell — 62

Christ Did Speak Against Homosexuality & Ungodly Politics — 65

Benefits of Marriage & What the Magna Carta Really Mean — 70

We Must Sacrifice Sin Like Christ Sacrificed Prosperity & His Whole Life — 72

God is Ashamed of People Who Do Not Stand for His Word — 74

People Who Live Godly in Christ Jesus Shall Suffer Persecution — 77

Political & Chronological Events that Led to Legalizing Gay Marriages — 81

People in the Southern Part of the USA Stand Against — 90

Homosexuality the Most Crucifixion of Christ by President Obama & Hypocrite Christians	92
Biden's Blasphemous, Hypocritical & Anti-God Comments	97
It is Impossible for Real Christians to Support Homosexuality	98
The Creator of All Things Did Not Create Anyone Gay	100
Christians Who Support Gays are Self-righteous & Antichrist	102
Christ's Word is Like a Sword and a Fire	104
Our Homes and Families Must Be Holy and Sanctified	110
Joel Osteen and Other Hypocrite Preachers Caused Death	112
Some Christians Pollute God's House of Worship	115
Our Bodies Are Temples of God, but God Does Not Dwell Inside Defiled Temples	118
God Does Not Dwell Inside Unclean Temples, but Demons Do	120
Gay Couples are Not Brides of Christ and Are Not One with Christ	122
Not All Sins Are the Same and God Punishes Some Sins Harder Than Other Sins	126
We Must Not Support Ungodly Politics Simply for Worldly Gain	130
Spirituality Supersedes Equality	133
Gay Animals	135
Some Black People Rejected God Because Obama Was Black	136
Black Peoples' Fight for Civil Rights Do Not Compare to the Fight for Gay Rights	138

Most Black People Do Not Want to Be Compared to Gays	140
Homosexuality is Fleshly and Demonic and is Against the Spirit of God	142
Gay Rights Came Easier Than Civil Rights Because Evil Loves Its Own People	144
Some People Support Gays Only for Money & Power	146
Bad & Evil Decisions by Leaders Cause Nations to Suffer	147
Christians Who Support Gays Are Calling God a Liar	151
Adoption of Children by Gay People Should Not Be Allowed	154
Muslims Do Not Support Gay Lifestyles as Much as Hypocrite Christians Do	156
Obama Caused People to Live by the Commandments of Man	158
Some People Idolized Obama and He Was Already an Antichrist	160
Obama Did Some Short-term Good but More Long-term Harm	164
We Must Be a Living Sacrifice After Christ Was a Crucified Sacrifice	166
Obama Was Not the Only Anti-God President	169
Gays Should Not Expect God to Think Like Them	171
It is Blasphemous to Say that Christ and the Apostles Were Gay	173
God's Punishment Nowadays is Harder Than That of Sodom and Gomorrah in the Past	175
People Have Reprobate Minds and Are Spiritually Blind Who Support Gays	179
People Are Not Judging When They Quote the Bible in Defense of God	181
Gays Are Sometimes Possessed with a Demon	183

Drag Queens and Cross-dressers	186
Hermaphrodites and Intersexuals	187
Transgenders, Gender Fluid, Transexuals, and Sex Changes	188
Adultery, Fornication, and Homosexuality Does Not Please God	190
Hope for Homosexuals	193
Aborting Innocent Babies is Crucifying Babies	195
Late-term Abortions and Partial-birth Abortions are Murders	199
Your Body Belongs to God, Not to You	201
Partakers and Supporters of Abortions are Also Punished by God	203
A Woman's Right to Choose	205
Guilt After Having an Abortion	207
When is the Wrong Time to Have a Child	208
Mercy and Forgiveness from God	210
Possible Punishment After Forgiveness	213
Abortions Are Crucifixions and Child Sacrifices unto the Devil	214
Government Financed Abortions	216
Abortion is an Evil Invention Created by Humans	219
Fornication and Adultery Causes Unwanted Pregnancies	221
Aborting Babies of Incest & Rape or to Save the Life of the Mother	223
The Hearts, Thoughts, and Actions of Abortionists	226
God is Life but He Punishes Murderers Terribly	228
COVID – 19 (Coronavirus)	230
References	235

About The Author	237
Books By This Author	239
Back Cover Summary	241

CHURCH PEOPLE WILL BE JUDGED FIRST BY GOD ON JUDGMENT DAY

One reason there are so many earthquakes, floods, and other forms of destruction in the world is because of Christians who do not obey the Word of God. Jesus did not come to save righteous people but sinners, because righteous people are already saved, though just barely saved. The Bible says that on judgment day, church people will be judged first by God and then the rest of the people will be judged by God and his angels, and by saved and sanctified humans and that if righteous people are barely saved, where shall the ungodly and the sinner appear (1 Pet. 4:12–19; Ezek. 9:6; 1 Cor. 3:5–17; Prov. 14:32; Matt. 12:41; 24:21–22)?

Willful and habitual sinners are in jeopardy of not inheriting the kingdom of God and will suffer on earth too (Rev. 21:8, 27; 22:14– 15; Mic. 2:1; Ps. 19:12–14; Rom. 1:18–32; 2 Thess. 2:10–15).

The Lord shall return on judgment day with ten thousand of his saints. That is a figurative number that includes not only angels but also saved and sanctified people who will help judge the world. The dead in Christ shall be resurrected first and return with Christ to judge the world (1 Thess. 4:13–18; Rev. 20:5–6; 1

Cor. 15:20–23).

Again, saved people shall return from heaven with God to judge ungodly people and people who have made ungodly comments about God. They are complainers, walking after their own lusts while having respect of persons and trying to impress people to gain advantage or admiration. The original apostles wrote that there shall be mockers in these last and evil days, who walk after their own ungodly lusts. They do not have the Spirit of God. But you, beloved, build yourself up in the faith while praying in the Holy Spirit, keeping yourself in the love of God, looking for the mercy of our Lord Jesus Christ unto eternal life. And on some people, we must have compassion, making a difference; but with others, we should save while being fearful for our own safety and resisting temptations, pulling them out of the fire of sin and suffering, and while hating their sins but loving the person. Now to Christ who is able to keep you from stumbling and to present you faultless to God our Savior, who alone is wise, be glory, dominion, power, and majesty, both now and forever. Amen (Jude 1:14–25; Gal. 6:1; Zech. 3:1–7; Matt. 17:14–21; Acts 19:14–18; Prov. 10:12; James 5:19–20; 2 Chron. 19:2–4).

A true witness of God delivers souls, but a deceitful witness speaks lies (Prov. 14:25). While truly being on a mission to save souls, you shall be protected by God like the person in the Old Testament when God rebuked Satan for trying to hinder that person who God said he had pulled out of the fire of sin and punishment (Zech. 3:1–7). But some people are plucked out of the fire by God, and they still will not return to him, so they must prepare to meet their Maker in God's wrath (Amos 4:10–13).

The fact that God says that righteous people scarcely go to heaven, that means that they have sinned too. But righteous people have hope in their death (Prov. 14:32). God has mercy on people who love and fear him (Exod. 20:6; John 15:14–15). That also means that those who love God have made mistakes, and Jesus also says if you love him, then obey the Word of God (John 14:15; Dan. 9:3–19). Most people will fall short of going to heaven (Titus 2:11– 12; Heb. 4:1; Matt. 7:13–14; Rev. 7:9; Luke 4:25–30; 13:23–24).

The Bible says, "Let them who think they stand take heed or they will fall too" (1 Cor. 10:1–14). People who endure until the end shall be saved (Matt. 10:20–22; 24:13; Heb. 3:7–19; John 6:26–29; Eccles. 9:11–12).

The eyes and ears are never satisfied and constantly seek sinful things (Eccles. 1:8; Luke 11:33–36). Therefore, the grave and hell are never satisfied and have enlarged itself and opened its mouth beyond measure (Job 24:19; Prov. 27:20; 30:15–16; Isa. 5:14). But heaven has been measured, because most people will not get in (Rev. 7:9; 21:10–17; Matt. 7:13–14; Luke 4:25–30; 13:23–24; 1 Pet. 4:17–18).

Jesus says that even if a dead person could return from hell to warn the world, they still would not take heed to the Word of God (Luke 16:19–31; Acts 13:41).

There is a scripture in the Bible that many people interpret as God allowing certain people to enter heaven, to talk to saved servants of God, and then be cast out into hell's fire (Matt. 8:11 – 12; Luke 13:24–28).

Most of the apostles forsook Christ and did not walk with him throughout his arrest, court trial, crucifixion, and execution (Mark 14:44–50; Matt. 26:30–31, 66–75).

Christ rose from the dead, and Thomas did not believe until he saw Christ and touched the nail holes in his hands, so Jesus told him, "Blessed are they who have not seen and still believe" (John 20:24–31). Christ says the apostles saw and heard things that prophets and kings did not see, but all of the holy prophets and some of the kings still believed (1 John 1:1–4; Acts 1:1–3, 8, 22; 2:32; 3:14–15; 4:18–20, 33; 5:28–29, 32; 10:39–48; 13:31; 22:14–18; 26:16; Luke 1:1–4; 10:23–24; 24:34–53; 1 Cor).

ADDING TO & TAKING FROM GOD'S WORD CAUSES SICKNESS & DEATH

There is a generation that is pure in their own sight and yet is not washed from their filthiness (Prov. 21:2; 30:12; Deut. 12:8). But David said that he loves God's Word and hates every false way and that the Word of God is right and very pure (Ps. 119:104, 128, 140; Hosea 14:9). If you add anything to the doctrine of God that is contrary to his true and pure Word, God will add diseases to your life. And if you take away from the Word of God, he will take your name out of the Book of Life, which means you go to hell, unless you repent (Deut. 4:2; 5:22; 12:32; Ezra 6:11; Prov. 30:5–6; Eccles. 3:14–15; Rom. 1:24–25; Rev. 22:18–19; 2 Pet. 3:16).

Everything and everyone that God did not plant shall be uprooted by the Lord and destroyed (Matt. 15:13; Acts 5:32–39; 1 Cor. 2:6).

HYPOCRITE PREACHERS & SOME POLITICIANS ARE THE WORSE PEOPLE ON EARTH

A lot of preachers hurt people by deceiving them and not teaching the whole truth about God, and most politicians work against God, and they also cause injustice and oppression while showing respect of persons (Luke 20:21; 1 John 4:1–6; James 2:1–4, 8; 1 Tim. 5:21; Deut. 10:17–22; Isa. 24:1–3; Col. 3:25).

A drug dealer for example, is not the worse person in the world, although they are among the worse people in the word. A drug dealer does indeed destroy families, lives, neighborhoods, and sometimes entire nations. But hypocrite preachers and weak preachers cause people's souls to be lost in hell, and some politicians cause people to die in unnecessary wars, and they turn a blind eye to oppression, genocide, racism, discrimination, slavery, poverty, unjust educational systems for minorities, unjust legal and prison systems, and corrupted politics. They legalized abortions killing millions of babies, and they legalized homosexuality and racial segregation while most citizens oppose those things.

Politicians are also the worse or second worse people in the world, second behind or tied for first with hypocrite and weak preachers, because politicians allowed cancer to kill millions of people. Cancer happened to most people because the government allowed companies to save money and make major profits by making almost everything in society with chemicals and preservatives that caused cancer, instead of making them with what God's earth produces like they were made for thousands of years before. Also, the government allowed farmers to grow and produce food with chemicals that cause cancer, including pesticides and herbicides. Politicians also allowed fake food to be produced. And cancer-causing plastic containers were allowed by the government because they increased shelf life and storage life of the products, resulting in millions of dollars in profits. Not to mention the fact that politicians allowed and assisted in global warming.

Most political systems do not like people and political candidates who have godly fear and desire to do right towards all people (Ps. 119:46–48; Jude 1:3). And a lot of preachers and politicians marry because it looks good in the church, in public, and in certain organizations and is sometimes a cover-up that is used to gain favor and respect.

Some of the best people in the world are sanctified and holy Christians, and even certain Christians who have just recently been baptized and converted are very good people, but some of the worst people in the world are so-called Christians, even some who claim to be devout, but do not profess to be sanctified, and there is a difference between being sanctified and being devout (2 Chron. 7:14; Matt. 13:14–15; Luke 19:37–42; Isa. 6:8–10; Lev. 26:3–6; 1 Kings 8:32–40; Deut. 29:26).

GOD HEALS THE LAND WHEN CHRISTIANS LIVE HOLY & SANCTIFIED

Sinners cannot expect to be saved while disregarding God's Word. When Christians do not obey God's Word, they fall under the following scripture: "If my people, which are called by my name, shall humble themselves, and pray, and seek my face, and turn from their wicked ways, then will I hear from heaven, and will forgive their sins, and will heal their land" (2 Chron. 7:14; Isa. 6:8–10; Ezek. 33:31; Matt. 13:14–15; Luke 19:37–42; Deut. 29:2–6).

God does not say, "If sinners and homosexuals repent," although they are required to repent, but God says that people who are called by his name must repent too. God also says the sinners of his people will die, along with the heathens who are called by his name (Amos 9:10). This means again that there are Christians who are hypocritical, and there are heathens who confess Christ but are still heathens (Amos 9:10). The Bible says, "My people are foolish. They have not known me. They are silly children, and they have no understanding. They are wise to do evil, but to do good they have no knowledge." God also says, "Great sorrow and distress will happen to people who call evil good, and good evil, who are wise and prudent in their own eyes. Who justify the wicked for money, and do not grant justice to righteous people. Therefore, as the fire devours the stubble, so their root will be as rottenness, because they have rejected the Word of God and the Holy One of Israel. Therefore, the anger of the Lord is aroused against his people. He has stretched out his hand against them and stricken them" (Isa. 5:20-25). David said to God, "When you say, seek my face, my heart said unto you, your face Lord, will I seek" (Ps. 27:8). Otherwise, God says, "I will go and return to my place until they acknowledge their sins, and seek my face, in their affliction they will seek me early" (Hosea 5:3-6, 15; Ps. 78:34).

When God punishes nations for their sins, even if people as righteous as Noah, Daniel, and Job were in those nations, they can only save themselves according to their righteousness, but their sons and daughters cannot go to heaven according to their parent's righteousness (Ezek. 14:12-20). Moses did get God to change his mind about destroying all the Hebrews in the wilderness for their sins, and Moses pleaded for their lives after they wanted to kill him two different times (Num. 14:10; Exod. 17:4). God told Jeremiah that the people of Israel could not get him to change his mind about punishing them even if Moses and Samuel stood before him to plead for them (Jer. 15:1-6). It is a sin to not pray for people, even for our enemies (1 Sam. 12:23; 1 Tim. 2:1-2; Matt. 5:44-45). But God told Jeremiah at one point to not pray for the sinful people of the land, because he would not hear his prayer (Jer. 7:16-20; 11:14; 14:11). And God tells all of us that there is a sin unto death and a sin not unto death and that we should not pray for the sin unto death, because God knows that we will not turn away from that sin. But the sin that God tells us to pray for is the sin that we repent for and turn away from (1 John 5:14-17; Jer. 7:16-20; 11:14; 14:11; Rev. 3:15-19; Matt. 12:33; Rom. 6:15-17; Ps. 66:16-20).

The Bible says, "If I regard iniquity in my heart, the Lord will not hear me. Blessed be the Lord who has not turned away my prayer, nor his mercy from me" (Ps. 66:18-20). The Bible also says that the Lord knows people who are his and to let everyone who confesses the name of Christ depart from sin (2 Tim. 2:19). Flee youthful lusts, and follow righteousness, faith, love, and peace with people who call on the Lord with a pure heart, always (2 Tim. 2:22; Job 27:8–23; Ps. 1; Prov. 3:5–8). The judgment of God starts at the church, with God's people (1 Pet. 4:17–18).

Jeremiah became discouraged and promised that he would not teach the Word of God anymore, but the Word was like fire in his bones, and he could not resist to teach the truth (Jer. 20:8–9). Jeremiah asked God, "Shall evil be repaid for good? They have dug a pit for my life. Remember that I stood before you to speak good for them, to turn away your wrath from them" (Jer. 18:20). Jeremiah said that he received affliction from God because of God's wrath on other people (Lam. 3:1–4). Those of you who are called by God's name, what are you going to do, stand for the Word of God or make excuses and lie on God (Ps. 119:46–47; Jude 1:3; Jer. 5:12)? We are justified by Christ, but Christ is not the minister of sin (Gal. 2:17). God asks, what sin have you found in him that causes you to sin (Jer. 2:5)?

FRIENDS OF THE WORLD ARE ENEMIES OF GOD

The United States, certain other nations, a lot of the media, some churches, and many organizations are anti-God. True religion is to go unspotted from the world (James 1:26–27). But the world loves its own people and not the people of God, and a friend of the world is an enemy of God (James 4:2–4; John 1:10–12; 15:18–19; 1 John 2:15–17; 3:13; Rom. 6; 8:1–16; Gal. 5:16–26; 1 Pet. 2:11; 1 Cor. 1:10; 2:9–16; Rom. 15:5–6; Phil. 3:16–21).

The Apostle Paul said that he was crucified from the world and the world from him (Gal. 6:14). Christ says, "I have overcome the world," and greater is Christ in you than they who are in the world (John 16:33; 1 John 4:4). Anyone can overcome the world too by being born again, but if after you have escaped the pollutions of the world and become entangled again with worldly matters, your latter end will be worse than the beginning (2 Pet. 2:20; 1 John 5:4–5). An unjust person is an abomination to righteous people, and righteous people are an abomination to the wicked (Prov. 29:27). Christians must not hate sinners including homosexuals, but they should hate sin, and it is not hateful or homophobic to hate people's sins while loving the person (Jude 1:14–25; Gal. 6:1; Zech. 3:1–7; Matt. 17:14–21; Acts 19:14–18; Prov. 10:12; James 5:19–20; 2 Chron. 19:2–4).

We are supposed to live in true holiness and righteousness "all the days of our life" (Luke 1:74–75; Eph. 4:21–32). Because it is written, be ye holy, for I am holy (1 Pet. 1:14–16; Eph. 4:21–32; 5:25 – 27; Rev. 20:6).

Also, the Holy Scripture says, "Let no one deceive you, they who live righteously are righteous, for God is righteous, and they who sin are of the devil (1 John 3:5–10). When you add another "o" to the word God, you get the word "good," but if you add the letter "d" to the front of the word "evil" you get devil, and we know the devil is evil. God is righteous, and everyone who strives to live right is born again (1 John 2:29; 3:7). We must put off anger, wrath, malice, blasphemy, and filthy words (Col. 3:8). God says, "I the Lord speak righteousness, I declare things that are right" (Isa. 45:19; Ps. 19:8). We must also be holy in all manner of conversation (1 Pet. 1:15; Ps. 19:12–14; Isa. 33:15–16; 1 Cor. 15:33; Eph. 4:21–32; Mal. 2:5–6).

GOD IS ALWAYS RIGHT BUT HUMANS ARE OFTEN WRONG

Nehemiah told God, "You are right in all that is brought upon us, for you have done right, but we have done wrong" (Neh. 9:33). David said, "Your righteousness O God, is very high, even though you have sent great trouble my way" (Ps. 71:19–20).

"Thus, says the Lord, 'Ask for the old paths, where is the good way, and walk therein, and you shall find rest for your souls. But they said, we will not walk therein'" (Jer. 6:16). The Prophet Jeremiah encountered women who idolized and led the practice of witchcraft. They along with their husbands told Jeremiah that they would not obey the word that Jeremiah had spoken in the name of the Lord. They went on to say that they would do whatever comes out of their mouth. Jeremiah then told them that God saw their evil sins and could no longer bear with them in their sins and abominations. And because they sinned against the Lord and did not obey the voice of the Lord, nor walked in righteousness, therefore evil happened to them.

Jeremiah went further by saying, "Hear the Word of the Lord, you and your wives have spoken with your mouths, and fulfilled with your hands, saying, we will surely keep our promises made against God. Therefore, hear the Word of the Lord, 'I have sworn by my great name, says the Lord, that my name shall no more be named in the mouth of anyone, saying, the Lord God lives. I will watch over you for evil, and not for good, and then you shall know whose words shall stand, God's, or yours. This shall be a sign unto you, says the Lord, that I will punish you in this place, that you may know that my words shall surely stand against you'" (Jer. 44:15–29).

The same applies toward any person who speaks against God and his Word, including people who support, embrace, and uphold homosexuality even though the Bible clearly speaks against homosexuality. Psalm 119:101 says, "I have refrained my feet from every evil way, that I might keep your Word." That is what every human should do. As for God, his way is perfect (Ps. 18:30).

WE DO & SUPPORT WHATEVER IS IN OUR HEART

We must receive the Word of God in our hearts after we hear it, and people usually do what is in their heart, because where your treasure is, there shall your heart be too (Ezek. 3:10; Luke 12:32–34; Rom. 2:6–11; 1 Kings 3:7–15; Heb. 11:24–27).

To clarify, whatever or whomever we desire, support, or believe in from the heart, we shall be with them and stand with them, whether it is God or a sinful human.

GOD CHASTISES WHO HE LOVES BUT REBELLIOUS PEOPLE ARE PUNISHED HARD

If God has chastised you, that means he loves you and has confidence in you doing his will, but also if you have been chastised by God and are still alive, that is even more evidence of his love for you (2 Cor. 6:9). God chastises people who he loves, and when our earthly parents chastise us, we show them reverence. So, shouldn't we be obedient to God and live? When God chastises us, it is for our profit, that we may go to heaven (Heb. 12:5–11). God loves us, but love does not rejoice in or support sin, but the truth (1 Cor. 13:6). If a person is not chastised by God, they are probably none of his and are spiritual bastards (Heb. 12:5–11; Rom. 8:9–11). For as many of you who have been baptized into Christ have put on Christ, were baptized into his death, and rose out of the water into newness of life (Gal. 3:27; Rom. 6:3–4). As Christ puts it, if you are not born of the water and of the Spirit, you cannot go to heaven (John 3:3–7; Acts 2:38–39; 8:14–17; 10:47–48; 19:2–5; Rom. 8:5–14).

ALL GOD'S CREATIONS DO WHAT HE MADE THEM TO DO EXCEPT MOST HUMANS

The main reason humans do not do exactly what God made us to do is because we have free will, and God wants us to have a choice—either choose him and do right while glorifying him or choose to do wrong while glorifying the devil, one another, or oneself. God made everything for his glory, but everything that God made glorifies him continually except humans as a whole (Ps. 148; Isa. 43:7, 20–22). Being gay or a lesbian is a matter of choice and not the way that God made them.

Birds fly and glorify God, fish swim, and glorify God, and the sun rises and sets while glorifying God. The Lord made mankind for his glory as well. God says, "Even everyone who is called by my name, for I have created them for my glory, I have formed them, yes, I have made them" (Isa. 43:7, 20–22). But God did not make anyone gay or lesbian, because that does not glorify him at all and would make God a liar, but it is impossible for God to lie, and God has never lied (Heb. 6:18; 1 John 2:27; Num. 23:19; Deut. 32:4; 1 Sam. 15:29; Ps. 89:35; 92:15; Jer. 15:18).

The devil is the father of lies, and homosexuality is a lie and not the truth (John 8:44). Christ says that the truth shall set you free and that his Word is truth. Christ also says that he sanctified himself so we too can be sanctified through the truth (John 8:31–36; 17:17–19; Isa. 29:23). To be sanctified is to be set aside and set apart for holy use, and being gay or lesbian is not sanctified or set apart for holy use. It is the devil's purpose to deceive the whole world (John 8:44; 12:31; 14:30; 2 Cor. 4:3 – 4; Luke 4:1 – 21).

If the devil cannot kill you and your loved ones, then he will certainly try to deceive you and keep you deceived until God destroys you for supporting sin. Then you would go to hell along with the devil and the lying ministers (Rev. 13:14; 20:8 – 10; John 10:10).

The Bible furthermore says, "Whether you eat, or drink, or whatsoever you do, do all to the glory of God, and for his pleasure" (Col. 3:17, 23; 1 Cor. 10:31; Eph. 1:9; Phil. 2:12–15; Heb. 13:21; Rev. 4:11).

"For of God, through God, and to God are all things, to whom be glory forever. Amen" (Rom. 11:36). But most of mankind does not do what God made us to do, which is to obey the Lord. And the Lord gives the Holy Ghost to people who obey him (Acts 5:32; Luke 11:13; John 1:1, 14; 14:13–18, 26–27; Col. 3:16; 1 John 2:5, 7, 14).

Christ also gives eternal salvation to people who obey him (Heb. 5:7–9). "'Christ the Redeemer shall come to people who turn from sin,' says the Lord" (Isa. 59:20). And God says, "How long will you turn my glory, which should be your body, to shame? How long will you love worthlessness and falsehood?" (Ps. 4:2). The Lord God Almighty says, "The ox knows its owner, and the donkey knows its master's crib, but most people do not know me, neither do they consider me" (Isa. 1:2–6; 43:20–22; Job 34:27). God speaks further by saying that birds know and obey God's will, but humans do not know the judgment of the Lord (Jer. 8:5–7). He also says, "A son honors his father, and a servant obeys their master. If then I be the Father, where is my honor? And if I be the Master, where is my fear?" (Mal. 1:6).

WE MUST LOVE & FEAR GOD AND NOT SIMPLY LOVE HIM

We must love, trust, and fear God and not simply love him for his goodness (Heb. 12:26–29; Isa. 66:1–2; Deut. 5:29; Exod. 20:20; Ps. 115:11; Prov. 22:4; 23:17; Mal. 2:5–6).

God takes pleasure in people who fear him and hope in his mercy (Ps. 147:10–11; 119:132). Therefore, although we must be wise enough to fear God, we all need mercy sometimes, and that is why God says that he has pleasure in people who fear him and hope in his mercy (Ps. 147:10– 11; 119:132).

If you say you fear God and obey his voice but still walk in darkness, you must evaluate yourself and truly trust in the Lord, rely on him, and obey him (Isa. 50:10; 2 Kings 17:20–41).

The beginning of wisdom is to fear God (Ps. 111:10). David loved the Lord and expressed it repeatedly when he wrote the book of Psalms, but scripture also says that David feared the Lord (1 Chron. 21:27–30). Obadiah (not the prophet) was a high-ranking officer for King Ahab and Queen Jezebel, but he feared God greatly instead of fearing the king and queen. Jezebel massacred some of God's prophets, but Obadiah hid one hundred of God's prophets from Jezebel (1 Kings 18:3–4). That is a perfect example of fearing God, serving God, and standing with God even while putting your own life in jeopardy, although most of us will not ever be faced with such a challenge for the Lord's sake. Therefore, the least we can do is stand with God against homosexuality and other sins. Jezebel even told Elijah that she planned to kill him in no more than twenty-four hours (1 Kings 19:1–2).

An Egyptian king asked the Israelite women to kill all male born babies to extinguish the Hebrew population, but the ladies feared God and not man, so God awarded them houses for their fear of him (Exod. 1:8–21). Not fearing God causes us to suffer on earth and fall short of heaven (Heb. 4:1; Deut. 28). The Bible says, "Let them who think they stand take heed or they will fall too" (1 Cor. 10:1–14). In every nation, people who fear God and work righteousness are accepted by God (Acts 10:35).

God is good and he does good toward us to try to draw us to repentance, and when it does not, trouble will eventually follow — but to people who obey God, eternal life, glory, honor, and peace, and there is no respect of persons with God, because we reap what we sow (Rom. 2:4–11; Gal. 6:7–10). By God's mercy and truth, our sins are forgiven, but we are to depart from sin because we fear God (Prov. 16:6). God is good, but that same good God will send some people to hell, and most people love hearing that God is good and that he does not punish us or that he does not punish us severely. However, God himself says that his goodness and easy punishments toward us do not cause us to fear or to obey him, but that it should (Isa. 57:11–13; Hosea 3:5). God says that he will forgive us and cleanse us of our sins if we allow him to do so, and when people hear the good that God does toward us, they shall "fear" God for his goodness and the prosperity that he provides (Jer. 33:8–9). Thus again, God's goodness and grace should not be taken for granted and should cause us to fear him. His goodness does not give us a free pass to be disobedient.

God is good, but how good are you to God? We were created to serve and to glorify God (Isa. 43:7, 20–22). God will say to obedient people on judgment day, "Well done, my good and faithful servant" (Matt. 25:23). "And you shall receive a crown of life," because those of us who are with Christ even in hard times and in times of persecution are called, chosen, and faithful, while being surrounded by anti-Christian practices of other people (Rev. 2:10; 17:14).

THE HOLY PROPHETS & APOSTLES WERE GREATER THAN PRESIDENT OBAMA

The Apostle Paul said concerning himself and the writings of the apostles who walked with Christ on earth, "Hold to the traditions that you have been taught, whether by our word or by our writings" (2 Thess. 2:15). A demon once told a man, "Christ I know, and Paul I know, but who are you?" (Acts 19:13–17). The same is to be said about people who try to discredit the Apostle Paul while justifying themselves, President Obama, or any human who rejects the Bible. Who are you? You have not experienced half of what the apostles experienced with Christ on earth and for Christ's sake?

Christ himself told the apostles that they shall bear witness of him, because they were with him from the beginning (John 15:27). John said that he bore record of Christ's teachings and deeds (Rev. 1:1–2; John 1:34). The apostles also ate and drank with Christ after the resurrection (Acts 10:40–41). The Bible tells us to mark people who are contrary to the Word of God (Rom. 16:17–19; Phil. 3:17). That is one reason Paul said, "Be ye followers of me, even as I also am of Christ, remember me in all things, and keep the ordinances as I delivered them to you" (1 Cor. 4:15–16; 11:1–3; Phil. 3:17). The life and writings of the apostles are our examples (Phil. 3:17; 1 Thess. 1:5–7). Paul also said, "You are saved, if you keep in memory what I preached unto you, otherwise you have believed in vain" (1 Cor. 15:1–2).

Christians sometimes talk about the comforting scriptures that say we should forget the things that are behind us and press toward the mark of the prize of the high calling of God in Christ Jesus (Phil. 3:13–14). But the rest of the chapter says, "Let us walk by the same rule, let us mind the same thing, for many are enemies of the cross of Christ, whose end is destruction, whose god is their belly, and whose glory is their shame, who mind earthly things. For our conversation is in heaven, and we look for the Savior, the Lord Jesus Christ, who shall change our body like his glorious body" (Phil. 3:16–21). And his body is not gay! The term belly in these scriptures refer not only to people eating food but also to greed and personal gain that comes from being disobedient to God. "In regard to homosexuality, when the Bible says that their glory is their shame, it is referring to people who are proud to be gay and who glorifies being gay, but they should be ashamed to be gay" (Phil. 3: 16–21). Another scripture says that they do not serve our Lord Jesus Christ, but their own belly, and by good words and fair speeches they deceive the hearts of the simpleminded (Rom. 16:17–18; Phil. 3:16–18; 2 Thess. 3:14; 2 Tim. 4:1– 5; Isa. 30:8–13; Jer. 5:30–31).

But again, it is impossible to deceive the elect Christian and the truly sanctified Christian (Matt. 24:24).

The Apostle Paul said, "My speech and my preaching was not with enticing words of man's wisdom but was a demonstration of the Spirit and of power" (1 Cor. 2:4). The apostles wrote about what they saw and heard while with Christ (1 John 1:1–4; Acts 1:1–3, 8, 22; 2:32; 3:14–15; 4:18–20, 33; 5:28–29, 32; 10:39–48; 13:31; 22:14–18; 26:16; Luke 1:1–4; 10:23–24; 24:34–53; 1 Cor. 9:1–2; Matt. 13:10–17).

ELIJAH PAUL

MARTIN LUTHER OF EUROPE & DR. MARTIN LUTHER KING, JR. WERE GREATER THAN PRESIDENT OBAMA

Christians must have the mind of Christ and Dr. Martin Luther King Jr. certainly did, but all Christians must have the mind of Christ while searching the deep things of God, because natural-thinking people cannot receive the things of the Spirit of God. Holy and sanctified Christians have not received the spirit of the world, but the Spirit of God, not as man's wisdom teaches us, but as the Holy Spirit teaches us, comparing spiritual things with spiritual (1 Cor. 2:9–16; Dan. 2:18–23, 47; Ps. 92:5).

Dr. Martin Luther King Jr. was a holy and sanctified Christian pastor and prophet who was one of the greatest humans in American history. Martin Luther of the Protestant Reformation of the sixteenth century in Europe was one of the greatest humans in European history. Dr. Martin Luther King Jr. was sent to us by King Jesus— Martin's last name was King, and Martin served the King named King Jesus. Barack Obama was not as great as Dr. Martin Luther King, Jr., and Pres. Barack Obama was not as great as the Apostle Paul and Moses who God used to write the scriptures that tell us that homosexuality is filthy in the sight of God. God thought so much of Moses that he talked to Moses from heaven and later allowed Moses to see him from behind, knowing that no man can see God face to face without dying (Exod. 3:1–6; 20:22; 25:17–22; 33:9–11; 17–23; Num. 1:1; 12:9–11; Lev. 1:1).

When God called Paul to the ministry, he talked to Paul directly and verbally (Gal. 1:12, 15–19; Acts 9:1–20). Thus, those two men who wrote against homosexuality were closer to God than any human being that we know. We must admit that Dr. Martin Luther King Jr. was one of the greatest Americans to ever live, but the only color black people, white people, and all people should be concerned with is the color of the blood of Jesus Christ, red. After Jesus died for us all, he made all nations one blood (Acts 17:26; 1 John 2:2–4; Heb. 2:9; Rom. 5:6–9). This means true Christians belong to the Christian race. Color, nationality, ethnic background, tribes, and political affiliation do not matter. All that matters is the Word of God.

PEOPLE SHALL BE UPROOTED WHO DO NOT PRODUCE GODLY DEEDS

Jesus says that we are the salt of the earth, but if salt loses its flavor, it is good for nothing and it is thrown out and trodden under the foot of humans (Matt. 5:13), just as vines and branches that do not produce good fruit are cast into the fire (Isa. 5:1–7; Ezek. 15; 19:10–14; Hosea 10:1–2).

Jesus was once hungry and wanted to eat, but when he saw a fig tree with no fruit, he cursed the tree for not producing fruit (Matt. 21:18–19). It was not doing what it was made to do, which was to produce fruit. He will curse us the same way according to the Bible (2 Pet. 2:14). Jude 1:12 says that some sinners are like trees whose fruit withers and are even without fruit, twice dead, plucked up by the root. John the Baptist said that if a tree does not produce, it should be cut down (Matt. 3:10–12). The seed to a prosperous spiritual life is the Word of God (Luke 8:11; 1 Pet. 1:23). Christ says that he is the true vine, we are the branches, and everyone who lives in Christ, and he in us, produces good fruit and is strengthened by Christ. But every branch that does not bear good fruit is taken away from living trees and burned for firewood because the branch is withered and dry (John 15:1–14; Jer. 5:10).

To know how to do good and refusing to do it is sin (James 4:17; Luke 12:41–48; Lev. 5:1; Prov. 3:27–29).

David was a man after God's own heart, and he sinned terribly, but he never rebelled against God; he repented and accepted his terrible punishment (2 Sam. 11; 12:1–24; 1 Kings 14:8; 15:3–5).

People who often talk about God being in their heart often use that as an excuse to not stand for the Word of God (Ps. 119:46–47; Jude 1:3). Heart without works is dead, just as faith without works is dead (James 2:13–26; Matt. 7:7; Mark 2:1–5). When we believe, we must also speak the truth about God (2 Cor. 4:13).

IF WE EXPECT GOD TO BLESS AMERICA, WE MUST BLESS & OBEY GOD

If you are a Christian and you support, allow, or go along with gay relationships and the fact that they can adopt children, then you are guilty of "the world loving its own and of being an enemy of God" (John 15:17–19; James 4:4). Those scriptures also say that heterosexuals who commit adultery are enemies of God (James 4:4; John 15:17–19).

Americans claim to be *one nation under God* and share the slogan "In God We Trust," but if they are to be *one nation under God*, they must stand with God and for God by proving that they trust in him in good times and hard times. God's wrath toward us is according to our fear toward him (Ps. 90:11). If people do not fear, respect, and have reverence for God, then God's anger and wrath become worse toward those people than toward people who do fear God but made a sinful mistake at some point. So when Christians support homosexuality as though they are not afraid of God, his wrath will be greater (Ps. 90:11).

Americans also share the song, slogan, and cliché, "God Bless America." If God is to bless America, Americans must first bless God by obeying the Bible. Considering all the sinful laws and practices that the American government has legalized, the national motto should be, "God Please Have Mercy on America," and "God Please Teach Us Your Ways" (Ps. 119:68). Presidents, politicians, celebrities, athletes, and citizens cursed God by speaking against his Word; but they have national days of prayer and say, "God bless America," in their speech. And when tragedies happen, they ask people to pray.

The Bible says that cursing and blessing should not come from the same mouth (James 3:10). Just as water fountains do not produce fresh water and saltwater, wise people with knowledge should show with good conversation their works with meekness of wisdom, without envying and strife, and they do not lie against the truth. Otherwise, that wisdom does not come from heaven, but from earth and the devil. But wisdom from heaven is first pure and without hypocrisy (James 3:8–18).

David and Solomon said that they will bless the Lord at all times, and that they would not lean unto their own understanding (Ps. 34:1; Prov. 3:5–10).

SOMETIMES GOD DOES NOT HEAR SINNERS' PRAYERS

God says that sometimes before we call, he will answer, and while we are yet speaking, he will hear, but this is in reference to people who pray to God sincerely (Isa. 65:24). The Bible says that God does not hear the prayers of sinners, but he does hear people who worship him and do his will (John 9:24–33; Ps. 66:16–20). Those are not the words of Christ but are words of a man who Christ healed after being born blind. The critics of Christ accused Christ of being a sinner, and they did not believe that the man was healed by Christ, so the man told them that if Christ was a sinner and not the Son of God, then how could he have healed a grown man who was born blind? Christ certainly was not a sinner who was too insincere to have his prayers answered by God. So the man who said that God does not hear sinners was not telling the truth (John 9:24–33), because God does hear sinners, whether he answers them or not (Job 8:20; 35:13; Ps. 66:16–20; Prov. 1:28–30; Isa. 1:15; 59:1–2; Mal. 2:17; Jer. 14:7–12).

The prayers of the righteous avails much (James 5:16). Sinners who humble themselves and admit their wrong are likely to be heard and answered by God (Luke 18:9–14; 23:39–46). That does not mean that God dwells with them daily, because God answers and dwells with people who are of a lowly spirit and contrite heart toward him and who trembles at his Word. As a result,

God will revive the spirit and heart of humble people who have a contrite heart (Isa. 57:15; 66:1–2; Ezra 9:6; 2 Cor. 7:9–10; Ps. 34:15–18; 38:15–18; 51:17; 85:8; Ezek. 18:21–22).

King Nebuchadnezzar of Babylon served God by leading his army against Tyre, and the Lord said that they labored tremendously without reward. But because all things and all people belong to God, even unsaved people, God rewarded him for punishing a people that God wanted to be punished. So Nebuchadnezzar was not saved, but God still blessed him with prosperity (Ezek. 29:17–21). But what profits a person to gain the whole world and lose their soul (Mark 8:36–37; Luke 12:4–5; James 1:8–27; Job 27:8–23)?

The Word of God is perfect, converting the soul (Ps. 19:7–8). And just as God used an unsaved and ungodly person in Nebuchadnezzar to punish another ungodly people, he now uses Muslim extremists to punish hypocrite Christians, and he even rewards them for their service to him just as he rewarded an unsaved and ungodly Nebuchadnezzar. Most Muslims are not extremists or terrorists, and not everyone is a hypocrite who dies by the hand of any extremist or terrorist.

In the book of Jeremiah, God says, "I listened and heard, but they do not speak right, no one repented of their sin and wickedness, saying, 'What have I done?'" (Jer. 8:6). The Bible says all unrighteousness is sin and that people should not pray about sins that they know they will continue to do, because God knows they will continue in those sins, even unto death, but there is a sin not unto death and it is the sin that people pray and repent for and stop committing (1 John 5:16–19). Even if they do not repent and turn from their sins, God may answer sinners in terms of necessities, wants, and help. But he does not hear the prayers of sinners at all when they claim to repent and do not plan to turn from their sins or at least ask God to help them turn from their sins (1 John 5:14–17; Jer. 7:16–20; 11:14; 14:11; Rev. 3:15–19; Ps. 66:16–20; Matt. 12:33; Rom. 6:15–17).

God knows if we are sincerely asking for help or not. When Jesus healed and delivered sinners in the Bible, he told them to go and sin no more, or a worse thing will happen to them (John 5:14; 8:3–11). So God's blessings shine on the just and the unjust, the good, the evil, and the unthankful (Deut. 9:4–7; 10:17–22; Ezek. 29:17–20; Matt. 5:43–48; Luke 6:35; Acts 14:8–18; Ps. 17:13–15; Neh. 9:35–39; Ps. 145:9–10).

When God gives to sinners, that does not mean that God is pleased with them. And on judgment day, you shall rise the way you died, either holy, just, unjust, or filthy; and you will be judged by God according to your works, actions, and deeds (Rev. 22:10–13).

In terms of asking for salvation, forgiveness, and eternal life, God does not hear us unless we truly repent with godly sorrow (2 Cor. 7:9–10). God will hear the prayers of helpless sinners if they confess their sins and put them in his hands, because they may be too weak to change on their own (Luke 18:9–14). But to be weak is one thing, and to be hard-hearted, stubborn, anti-God, and self-justifying is a different evil. Jesus says, "Pray that you enter not into temptation, and that the spirit is willing, but the flesh is weak" (Matt. 26:41). At least weak Christians who admit their wrong are willing to pray and serve the Lord instead of being anti-God, hard-hearted, stubborn, and self-justifying. But yet again, God will help sinners who are too weak to change, if they sincerely want God to deliver them from what they are too weak to change on their own. They, who the Son of God set free, are free indeed (John 8:34–36; Rom. 6). Where the Spirit of Christ is, there is freedom (2 Cor. 3:17).

David said, "I cried unto God with my mouth. If I regard sin in my heart, the Lord will not hear me. But God has heard me, he has attended to the voice of my prayer. Blessed be God who has not turned away my prayer, nor his mercy from me" (Ps. 66:16–20). God told Job's friends that he would hear Job's prayers concerning them, but that he would not hear their prayers, because Job was righteous, and they spoke incorrectly about God

(Job 4:1–8; 32:1–10; 34:34–37; 42:7–9).

God reaches out his hands daily to a rebellious people, but they walk after their own thoughts (Isa. 65:1–2). God made everyone upright, but mankind has created so many evil inventions and many people shall die because of the evil inventions (Eccles. 7:26–29; Ps. 33:13–15; 99:8; Rom. 1:21–32).

That is why God repented for making humans, because even though he made us righteous, our imagination is evil from our youth, due to the evil inventions of mankind (Gen. 8:21; Jer. 32:30; Ps. 106:29, 39–48).

However, God will not repent for saving people who live holy and righteous (Hosea 13:14).

OBAMA NATION BECAME ABOMINATION

King Josiah in the Bible removed all abominations from the land and the people served the Lord God until Josiah died (2 Chron. 34:33). President Obama as leader of the United States did not take abominations out of the land but added even more evil abominations. The United States became an "Obama-nation" and an "abomination." After he left office, he stated in April 2017 that he failed to unite the United States. A person does not have to be a Harvard graduate to know that he could not unite a nation by allowing gays to marry and to adopt children and allowing transgender people to use the restrooms of their choice and to share locker rooms with either gender. That is totally unacceptable, and it is a disgrace and even dangerous for a person of the opposite sex to use the locker rooms and restrooms of people who were born male or female. The Bible even mentions a women's quarters that only women could enter while they dressed and that men waited outside until the ladies exited the women's quarters (Esther 2:3, 11, 13). Natural-born female athletes are rightfully in disapproval of males who participate in female sporting events, breaking female records, because they are males who participate as transgender females. That too is a disgrace and very unfair to natural-born female athletes.

The very first chapter and the very first verses of the book of Psalms says, "Blessed is the person who walks not in the counsel of the ungodly, nor stands in the paths of sinners, but their delight is in the law of the Lord, and in God's law they meditate day and night" (Ps. 1:1–2). The earth mourns and fades away, people are growing weak and feeble, and the earth is defiled, because the inhabitants have transgressed God's Word and changed his ordinances and covenants. Therefore, the curse has devoured the earth, and those who dwell on it are desolate (Isa. 24:4–6). The Bible says, "In the last days dangerous times have come. For people shall be lovers of themselves, covetous, boasters, proud, blasphemers, despisers of things that are good, traitors, high-minded, lovers of pleasures more than lovers of God, having a form of godliness, but denying the power thereof. Ever learning, and never able to come to the knowledge of the truth" (2 Tim. 3:1–7). They wrestle with Holy Scriptures to their own destruction (2 Pet. 3:14–18). The acceptance of homosexuality in societies nowadays is perfectly described in the Holy Scriptures, and it has contributed to causing dangerous times (2 Tim. 3:1–7).

The original apostles said that if the Word of God is hidden, not revealed, or not understood, it is hidden to people who are lost, in whom the god of this world has blinded the minds of people who believe not the Word of God, especially the New Testament (2 Cor. 4:3–4). The Lord says that we must live by every Word of God (Luke 4:4; Exod. 24:7; Deut. 4:1–9; 8:3).

Anyone who wants to hear the truth will hear the whole truth of God (John 18:37; Luke 4:4; Exod. 24:7; Deut. 4:1–9).

After God sent Jeremiah to warn the people, God eventually told Jeremiah that the people could choose to return to him, but he must not return to them (Jer. 15:19). To God, people who turn their ears away from hearing his Word, their prayer becomes an abomination to God, but the prayer of righteous people is a delight to God (Prov. 28:9; 15:8; 19:21).

The truth is evil spoken of, but people run with itching ears to hear a lie or something that is ungodly and unholy (2 Tim. 4:1–4; 2 Pet. 2; Jude 1; Prov. 17:3–4).

The disciples asked Christ why did he speak to the people in parables. Jesus replied and said that true followers of Christ are given the mysteries of the kingdom of heaven, but to nonbelievers and those who do not believe the whole Word of God, it is not given. For whosoever accepts the truth, to them shall more be given, but whomever does not accept the whole Word of God, Christ shall take away what they already have (Matt. 13:10–12). Jesus uses parables because a lot of people look and hear but do not see, do not listen, and do not understand. Their ears are tired of hearing the Word of God and they have closed their eyes, otherwise they would understand with their heart, be converted, and be healed from sickness and sin by Jesus Christ (Matt. 13:13–16). Again, the Word of God is hidden to people who are lost (2 Cor. 4:3–4). But Jesus says, "There is nothing hid or secret, which shall not be made known. If anyone has an ear to hear, let them hear. Take heed to what you hear, for they who have the Word of God shall receive more, but they who reject the Bible shall lose the godly knowledge that they did have" (Mark 4:22–25). Jesus says, "They who have ears to hear, let them hear" (Matt. 11:15; 13:9–16, 43; Luke 8:4–8; Rev. 2:7; 3:6, 20–22; Isa. 6:8–-13; 29:9–14; Ezek. 3:26–27; Deut. 29:2–6).

PERSECUTION FOR STANDING WITH GOD AGAINST HOMOSEXUALITY

Homosexuality is the act and process of having, or desiring to have, a sexual or intimate relationship with a person of the same sex. According to the Holy Bible, this is a deadly sin and is of the devil (1 John 3:8–10; Rom. 6:23). Notice that one of those scriptures says, "Whosoever does unrighteousness is not of God, nor are they who do not love their brother or sister" (1 John 3:8–10). Brother and sister, this instance means people in general. So to hate a homosexual is a deadly sin as well. The Lord says that the Word of God is foolishness to the natural minded person because they are not spiritually minded (1 Cor. 2:14–16). When you stand against homosexuality, people of the world would call you homophobic, but that is not true. You are standing with God and for God. "Blessed are they who are persecuted for righteousness' sake, and all manner of evil is spoken against them falsely for Christ's sake. Rejoice and be exceedingly glad, for great is your reward in heaven, for so they persecuted the holy prophets who were before you" (Matt. 5:10–12; Ps. 38:15–22). Paul said that sanctified children of God both labor and suffer reproach because they trust in the living God (1 Tim. 4:10). Jesus is despised and rejected, and he is acquainted with sorrow and grief (Isa. 53:3). With much wisdom also comes much grief (Eccles. 1:18). Isaiah 59:15 says that people who stand for the truth and depart from evil are attacked by sinners and the Lord sees it and is displeased with the attackers.

God himself says that when you stand for his Word and people despise you for it, they do not despise you, but they despise God, because you stand for God, and that God has not called anyone to uncleanness, but to holiness, and that we must love one another (1 Thess. 4:7–9). "Be steadfast, unmovable, always abounding in the work of the Lord, knowing that your work is not in vain in the Lord" (1 Cor. 15:58).

The Apostle Paul told Timothy to command and teach and to let no one despise him, but to be an example to the people (1 Tim. 4:11–12). Paul also told Titus to rebuke with all authority and to let no one despise you (Titus 2:15). Jesus and Paul both said that when people despise you for telling the truth, they really despise God (Luke 10:16; 1 Thess. 4:8). During the days of the Prophet Jeremiah, certain people told him that they would not listen to the word that he had spoken to them in the name of the Lord. And God responded by saying that he will see whose word will stand, His or theirs (Jer. 44:16, 28–29). God told the Prophet Ezekiel that the people will gather to hear him like they do in churches nowadays and they will enjoy the music, but they will not obey the Word of God that he preached (Ezek. 33:30–33). Some people gather to feast, drink wine, and play music on several different kinds of instruments, but they do not regard the work of the Lord, nor do they consider the operation of his hands; therefore, the grave and hell has opened its mouth wide (Isa. 5:11–14). The book of Isaiah also says,

> "And there is no one who calls on your name, who stirs themselves up to take hold of you. For you have hidden your face from us and have consumed us because of our iniquities. But now, O Lord, you are our Father. We are the clay, and you are the potter. We are all the work of your hands. Do not be

angry, O Lord, nor remember our iniquities forever. Please look. We all are your people" (Isa. 64:7–9).

HOMOPHOBIA & ABOMINATION

Some people say you are homophobic and hateful when you stand for God, but according to the Bible, people who justify sinners and condemn the righteous are abomination to the Lord, just as homosexuality is an abomination (Prov. 17:15). An abomination is a person or thing that is vile, disgusting, detestable, impure, and shameful. The Bible says that all workers of abomination go to hell if they do not repent and do the will of God, but so do liars, murderers, idolaters, workers of sorcery, people who do not believe in Christ, and heterosexual fornicators and adulterers; but abomination is a sin that is totally disgusting to God (Rev. 21:8, 27; 22:14–15). Even before certain people die, God punishes them without pity, according to their ways and their abominations (Ezek. 7:5–11). God is jealous, and he gets revenge on people who act or speak against him. The Lord is slow to anger, and he will not acquit the wicked. "The Lord is good, a stronghold in the day of trouble, and he knows people who trust in him, but darkness shall pursue his enemies. What do you imagine against the Lord? He will make an utter end, affliction will not rise a second time" (Nah. 1:1–3, 7–9). Sinful things that are highly esteemed among mankind are abomination to God (Luke 16:15). "An unjust person is an abomination to righteous people, and righteous people are an abomination to the wicked" (Prov. 29:27). If Christians hate the sin and not the sinner, they are not homophobic nor transphobic (Jude 1:14–25; Gal. 6:1; Zech. 3:1–7; Matt. 17:14– 21; Acts 19:14–

18; Prov. 10:12; James 5:19–20; 2 Chron. 19:2–4).

SUPPORTING HOMOSEXUALITY IS TO HATE & REJECT GOD

The Bible's definition of love tells us to stand with our loved ones unto death, but that same definition says that love does not rejoice in sin, but in God's truth (1 Cor. 13:6). People who find their worldly life shall lose their natural life, but they who lose their worldly life for Christ's sake shall find their spiritual life (Matt. 10:34–39; 1 John 5:12). "The wicked shall be turned into hell, and all the nations that forget God," and God shows ungodly leaders of all nations that they are only flesh and blood (Ps. 9:16–20).

The Bible says, "People who love the Lord hate evil" (Ps. 97:10). The fear of the Lord is to hate evil, pride, arrogance, and the evil way. And God says, "I love people who love me, and people who seek me early shall find me" (Prov. 8:13–17). Paul tells us to withdraw from people who do not obey Christ, the prophets, and the apostles and to not hate them, but warn and caution them (2 Thess. 3:6–15). David wrote, "Let people who fear the Lord turn to me, people who know his Word. I am a companion with people who fear God, and with people who obey the Word of God" (Ps. 119:63, 79). Be sure your love is true while hating what is sinful and holding on to what is good (Rom. 12:9). Jesus says, "Whosoever shall do the will of my Father who is in heaven, the same is my brother, and sister, and mother" (Matt. 12:46–50; Mark 3:31–35).

Homosexuals and any sinner who is hard-hearted against God are not the brothers and sisters of Christians because they are not doing the will of God, which is in heaven, unless they repent and change their ways (Matt. 12:46–50; Acts 2:38). If the sinner does not repent, there shall be no reward for them, and their candle shall be put out (Prov. 24:20). Some gay people say that if being gay increases their chances of going to hell, then they still will not change. This is no surprise, because God knows everything, past, present, and future (Ps. 147:5; Prov. 3:19–20; 2 Sam. 12:7–14; Job 31; Jer. 16:17; Deut. 31:14–23).

When homosexuals and any sinner repent and turn away from their sins, all of heaven rejoices (Luke 15:1–10). Therefore, we must not hold their past against them if they become a new creature and are born again, because "old things are passed away, and all things are new" (John 3:3–7; Rom. 8:5–14; 2 Cor. 5:16–17). Christians must not hate any sinner but love the sinner and hate their sin (Jude 1:22–24; James 5:19–20; Prov. 8:13; 10:12; Ps. 97:10; 101:3; 119:128; Gal. 6:1; Am. 5:14–15).

GOD'S JUDGMENT ON HYPOCRITE CHRISTIANS & NONBELIEVERS

On judgment day, we will rise the way we died. The Bible says, "They who are unjust, let them be unjust still; they who are filthy, let them be filthy still; they who are righteous, let them be righteous still; and they who are holy, let them be holy still. And behold, I come quickly, and my reward is with me, to give everyone according to their works" (Rev. 22:10–13; Acts 24:15; 1 Pet. 3:18; Dan. 12:1–3; Ezek. 18:19–32; 2 Thess. 1:4–12).

On judgment day and on the day of their death, it will be too late for the unjust, unthankful, and the evil to change and join Christ (Rev. 22:10–13), because there will be a resurrection of the dead, of both the just and the unjust (Acts 24:15). Holy and just people shall forever remain holy and just, but unjust and filthy people shall forever remain unjust and filthy (Rev. 22:10–13). All dead humans shall rise—some to everlasting life in heaven and some to everlasting pain and suffering in hell (Dan. 12:1–3; Matt. 13:47–50; 25:31–46; Acts 24:15; John 5:24–29).

God certainly blesses and protects his servants, even until old age and death, and he bears them, because he made them (Isa. 46:4). God, in his grace and mercy, blesses ungodly people, but they still make plans against him (Hosea 7:15). So God gives blessings to the just and the unjust, the good, the evil, and the unthankful, because they are his creation too, but being blessed with earthly possessions does not mean that any person is saved (Deut. 9:4–7; 10:17–22; Ezek. 29:17–20; Matt. 5:43–48; Luke 6:35; Acts 14:8–18; Isa. 57:15–21; 64:4–8).

WE MUST BE LIKE GOD TO PLEASE GOD BUT GOD IS NOT GAY

In heaven, we shall see God like he is, and we shall be like him (Phil. 3:17–21; 1 John 3:2; Ps. 17:14–15).

But we cannot be like him in heaven if we do not strive to be like him on earth (Titus 2:11–15; Matt. 6:10). When we see God like he is, and when we become like him in heaven, he and we will not be gay (1 Cor. 6:9–11; 1 Tim. 6:9–10; James 3:13–16; 2 Kings 5:15–27).

We were made in the image of God (Isa. 43:7, 20–22; Gen. 1:26; 1 Cor. 11:7; 15:47–55; Phil. 2:6–11; James 3:9). And the image of God does not consist of men with men, women with women, cross-dressers, transgenders, or same-sex couples with adopted children.

GAYS ADOPTING CHILDREN IS TO TRAIN CHILDREN IN AN UNGODLY WAY

The Bible says train a child in the way that they should go, in the Lord, and when they are older, they will not depart from it (Prov. 22:6). But when gays are allowed to adopt kids, the kids see a filthy and evil example by their gay adoptive parents, and the kids may be trained to be gay themselves, even molested, and may not depart from it when they are older.

Gay couples cannot conceive children because God made it impossible for them to do so. Some gay people want their names on the adopted children's birth certificate. That too should not be granted because they did not birth the children into the world. There were people in the Bible who were barren and could not have children, but they prayed to God for the ability to conceive and birth children. But nowadays, people who are totally capable of having children are failing to do so because they are in same-sex relationships and are adopting kids because it is impossible to conceive a child in those anti-God, filthy, and twisted relationships. There are also women nowadays who had the ability to conceive children, but they had abortions and/or used birth control for so long or used high health risk birth control to the point that they can no longer conceive a child, not to say that all forms of birth control are wrong.

THE TRIBES OF ANCIENT ISRAEL FOUGHT A WAR AGAINST HOMOSEXUALITY

It was homosexuality that initially caused the twelve tribes of Israel to separate and go to war against one another, and homosexuality in these scriptures is described as wickedness (Judg. 19:22–29; 20). Eleven of the tribes valued God's Word so much that they went to war against the one tribe that supported homosexuality. People all over this world should join to fight a spiritual war against the people who are gay and who support gays. But that will not happen because although the church body of Christ is strong, many church houses and congregations are weak and do not stand against sin. Notice how the eleven tribes stood together as one against homosexuality and sin (Judg. 20:1, 8, 11) and the gay men were called sons and children of Belial, which means wicked or sons and children of the devil (Judg. 19:22; 20:13). Finally, notice which of the eleven tribes God sent out to fight first against the supporters of homosexuality. The tribe of Judah went out first to fight—which is the tribe of Jesus, David, Joseph, Mary the mother of Jesus, Caleb, Daniel, and Shadrach, Meshach, and Abednego (Num. 34:19; Judg. 20:18;

Matt. 2:6; Luke 1:27; 2:4; 1 Sam. 16:1; 17:12; Dan. 1:6–7).

The tribe of Judah symbolized a lion (Gen. 49:9). And Jesus is the Lion of Judah (Rev. 5:5).

Even nowadays, when you serve sin or serve humans, you are serving the devil while making the ones you obey into an idol (Rom. 6:15–23; 1 Cor. 6:12–20; Col. 3:1–11; John 8:37–59).

The Bible says, "They chose new gods, then there was war, famine, and disease" (Judg. 5:8; 2 Chron. 16:9; Ezek. 14:13–23).

NATIONS ARE PUNISHED TERRIBLY BY GOD FOR HOMOSEXUALITY

Any nation that accepts gay marriage and the adoption of children by gay people will suffer from terror and violence, because there is no truth or knowledge of God in the land, and that is why God has a controversy with the inhabitants of the land (Hosea 4:1). That is also why Psalm 119:126 says, "It is time for you, Lord, to work, for they have made void your law." The law of the land allowed gays to adopt children before most states allowed them to marry. Just as one lie leads to another, one anti-God law leads to another. A little yeast causes the whole lump of dough to rise, and a little sin causes the whole sick government to sin even more (1 Cor. 5:1–6). But if the first fruits be holy and sanctified, then the whole lump of dough or whole body is holy (Rom. 11:16–25; Rev. 2:1–5; Jer. 50:6).

Those same scriptures highlight what terrible things happen to people who do not return to their first love, who is Christ. Nations that serve the Lord in righteousness are great, but sin is a shame to any people (Prov. 14:34). We are partakers with Christ, if we hold the beginning of our confidence steadfast unto the end (Heb. 3:14; Rev. 2:2–5; Matt. 13:1–23).

When a person, people, or nation depart from serving God, they are being a whore who is committing spiritual adultery against God, and God says that after he afflicts them for their sin, they will seek him early (Hosea 1:2; 5:15; Ps. 78:34). As God has destroyed other nations, he says he will also destroy this nation, because people are not obedient to his Word (Deut. 8:20).

Most Christians have heard that homosexuality is one reason that God destroyed the cities of Sodom and Gomorrah. But what most people do not know is that gay men in those cities tried to rape angels who they thought were human males. The angels blinded them and then destroyed them and the whole city (Gen. 19:1–13). This is why gays are sometimes called Sodomites (Deut. 23:17; 1 Kings 14:24; 15:12; 22:46; 2 Kings 23:7).

And God said that Sodom and Gomorrah were destroyed not only for homosexual acts but also for fornication and adultery between heterosexuals (Jude 1:7). The Bible warns us that some of us have entertained angels without knowing it (Heb. 13:2). While Lot, Abraham's nephew, lived in Sodom, his righteous soul was vexed, and he grieved over the sins and filthy conversations that he witnessed there. The Bible tells us that God turned Sodom and Gomorrah into ashes and condemned them, making them an example unto us who might live ungodly (2 Pet. 2:6–8). And in the New Testament, Christ suffered for us, leaving us an example, that we should live righteously like him (1 Pet. 2:21). Also, being children of God, if we want to share Christ's glory, we must also share his suffering (Rom. 8:16–17).

As stated earlier, Christ is acquainted with sorrow and grief (Isa. 53:3). And the Bible tells us, "With much wisdom comes much grief, and they who increase knowledge also increase sorrow" (Eccles. 1:18). Lot was wise, so he knew to grieve about the homosexuality that he witnessed.

God Almighty says that if a nation repents and turns from their evil, he will change his mind and not send evil their way, but if they do not obey God, he will change his mind about sending good to the nation (Jer. 18:8–10). God says regarding anti-Christian nations, "A sinful nation, a people laden with sin, a seed of evildoers, children who are corrupters, they have forsaken the Lord, they have provoked the Holy One of Israel unto anger, they are gone away backwards, the whole head is sick, and that if the Lord had not allowed some of us to live, our cities too would have been like Sodom and Gomorrah" (Isa. 1:4–9). Christians must be blameless and harmless children of God without rebuke, shining like a light in the world, in the midst of a crooked and perverted nation (Phil. 2:15; Deut. 32:4–5). We are the children of God only if we obey him and when we are holy, sanctified, and separate from the world (Acts 5:32; Luke 11:13; John 14:13–18, 26–27; Phil. 2:15; 1 Pet. 1:13–17; Rom. 8:1, 5–14; 2 Cor. 6:17–18; Deut. 32:4–5).

In the Old Testament and the New Testament, God's laws have always been different from worldly laws, and God's people are persecuted for living according to his Word (Esther 3:8; Acts 16:20–21; 17:6–7; Deut. 4:7–8).

In times past, God allowed all nations to walk in their own ways while he often gave them rain, food, and gladness, but now Christ requires everyone everywhere to repent (Acts 14:16–17; 17:30–31; Rev. 2:5, 16, 21–22; 3:3, 19).

However, in times past and in this present time, God sometimes withholds rain from certain nations and from certain parts of nations, and God sends other problems too, because they have not repented and turned away from their sins (1 King 8:35–40). The acceptance of gay marriage also causes floods, earthquakes, volcanoes, hurricanes, famines, tsunamis, mudslides, sinkholes, and other so-called natural disasters, which are often spiritual disasters and not simply natural disasters (Lev. 18:24–30; Matt. 24:7–8).

BIBLE STRICT & SPECIFIC SCRIPTURES AGAINST HOMOSEXUALITY

God Almighty says,

> "Thou shalt not lie with mankind, as with womankind, it is abomination. Defile not yourselves in any of these things. Doing so causes the land to be defiled. Therefore, I do visit the sin thereof upon it, and the land itself vomited out her inhabitants. You shall therefore keep my statutes and my judgments, and shall not commit any of these abominations, so the land spit not you out also, when you defile it, as it spat out the nations that were before you. The souls who commit them shall be cut off from among their people. Therefore, you shall keep my ordinance, that you commit not any one of these abominable customs, that you defile not yourselves. I am the Lord your God" (Lev. 18:22–30; 20:22).

The Bible says, "All people will walk in the name of their god, but we will walk in the name of the Lord our God forever and ever" (Mic. 4:5). That was in the Old Testament and before Christ died and rose from the dead. But nowadays, God is requiring all people everywhere to repent or face a strong possibility of dying sooner than later and going to hell (Luke 24:46–49; Acts 14:8–18; 17:26, 29–31). Jesus says that he will spit us out of his mouth if we are lukewarm and that he rather we be hot or cold. This means if you are hot for the Lord, he knows that you are his, and if you are cold, he knows that you are not (Rev. 3:15–19; 1 John 5:14–17; Matt. 12:33; Rom. 6:15–17).

We cannot straddle the fence. We must be on fire for the Lord after we confess and believe, but if we are cold or lost, Christ seeks us to save us, but to only confess and believe is to be lukewarm. Jesus also says, "Either make the tree good and its fruit good, or make the tree corrupt and its fruit corrupt, because a tree is known by the fruit it produces" (Matt. 12:33). But Christians who support homosexuality are lukewarm and attempting to serve God and support homosexuality at the same time. That causes people to be spit out of God's mouth (Rev. 3:15–16). Again, you must be hot for the Lord or cold and not with God at all—there is no lukewarm, there is no in-between, and there is no straddling the fence (Rev. 3:15–16).

Before Christ died for the sins of everyone, people were immediately put to death for being gay (Lev. 20:13). Jesus died so all people would not immediately die after they sin, but to have time to repent and live forever (Rev. 2:18–29; Rom. 5:9).

The New Testament's objection to homosexuality states,

> "God gave them up to uncleanness through the lusts of their own hearts, to dishonor their own bodies between themselves. Who changed the truth of God into a lie, and worshipped and served the creature more than the Creator, who is blessed forever, Amen.
>
> For this cause, God gave them up unto vile affections, for even their women did change their natural use into that which is against nature. And

likewise, also the men, leaving the natural use of the woman, burned in their lust one toward another, men with men. And even as they did not like to retain God in their knowledge, God gave them over to a reprobate mind. They are haters of God, despiteful, proud, boasters, inventors of evil things, disobedient to parents, and without understanding. Who knowing the judgment of God, that they which commit such things are worthy of death, but they continue to do those things, and approve of others who do them" (Rom. 1:18–32; 2 Thess. 2:10–15; 8:13–14; 1 Pet. 2:6–8; 2 Cor. 13:5; 2 Tim. 3:1–8; Titus 1:16).

The Bible also says, "I gave them up unto their own heart's lust, and they walked in their own counsels" (Ps. 81:12–16). Another New Testament scripture says that homosexuals cannot go to heaven (1 Cor. 6:9).

THE PRICE OF SIN IS DEATH BUT PUNISHMENT STILL HAPPENS BEFORE DEATH

In April of 2018, an American gay rights attorney committed suicide by setting himself on fire in protest. Firstly, Christ died for all people's sins and the death of anyone other than Christ cannot save us (1 John 2:2–4; Acts 17:26; Heb. 2:9; Rom. 5:6–9; 8:32; Isa. 53; John 11:47–57; 2 Cor. 5:15; Acts 10).

Secondly, the attorney was already sinning against God by supporting gay rights, but he died in even more sin by killing himself. Thirdly, it could have been the devil who convinced the man to kill himself while knowing that the man would go to hell for his act.

Christ still suffers when he sees our actions and his long-suffering and patience gives us time to repent, but to twist or reject the Bible brings about people's own destruction (2 Pet. 3:15–18). Just as during the Passover, blood placed over the doors of God's people in the Old Testament prevented God from killing their sons, the blood of Jesus prevents God from killing us nowadays when God passes over our lands and prisons, giving us time to repent (Exod. 12:5–7, 12–13; 1 Cor. 5:7; Rom. 5:9; 6:14–15, 23; Rev. 2:18–29).

Notice that Rom. chapter 6 ends by saying the price of sin is death, but it also begins by saying that grace does not allow us to continue in sin. Jesus speaks of a tower that fell on eighteen people who were not the greatest sinners, and he went on to say that unless greater sinners repent, they shall likewise perish (Luke 13:4–5). And in the Old Testament, God allowed a person to be buried in a dignified manner because he had some good in him, while others were not buried at all, but due to sin, that person still died just like the others (1 Kings 14:9–13). The Bible says, "Let them who think they stand take heed, or they too will fall" (1 Cor. 10:1–14). But when we truly repent, we repent unto life (Acts 11:18), because godly sorrow causes repentance unto salvation, but worldly sorrow causes death (2 Cor. 7:9–10; Ps. 38:15–18; 85:8; Ezek. 18:21–22).

Therefore, true repentance also gives us life everlasting in heaven (Gal. 6:7–8; Matt. 19:29; Luke 14:26–27; 18:29–30; Deut. 33:9).

Righteousness delivers us from death (Prov. 10:2; 11:4). That is why King Solomon said that the way of the righteous leads to life but the way of the unrighteous to sin and their own death (Prov. 10:16; 11:19). The prophet Hosea said, "Who is wise? Let them understand these things. For the ways of the Lord are right. Righteous people walk in them, but sinners stumble in them" (Hosea 14:9). In all your getting, get understanding of the Lord (Prov. 4:7; Jer. 9:23–24). God says that if we turn from our sins and do what is right, we shall surely live and not die (Ezek. 18:21).

Therefore, the price of sin was death in the Old Testament, and the price of sin is death in the New Testament, but it may take a little longer to die in the New Testament (1 Tim. 5:24; Mark 1:15; Matt. 4:17; Acts 2:38).

We are justified by Christ, but Christ is not the minister of sin (Gal. 2:17). Has God ever set a poor example for us by sinning himself (Jer. 2:5; John 34:46)? The answer is an obvious no!

When Christ told the woman who was caught in adultery that she was forgiven, he also told her, and other sinners, "Sin no more or a worse thing will happen to you" (John 5:14; 8:3–12). Some people ask why the Jews did not attempt to kill the man who was caught in adultery with the woman, as the law permitted for adultery and losing one's virginity (Lev. 20:10; Num. 5:27; Deut. 22:20–22; Ezek. 16:25–34). Maybe he had already been stoned to death, maybe he had not been found or brought forward yet, or maybe he was not mentioned because possibly certain men were neglectful when they translated the Bible into different languages. We do know that David was a man who committed adultery with a married woman, and God punished David by killing his newborn son and by allowing David's adult son to force him into exile. David would have been killed by his son who did temporarily take all of David's possessions, including the entire kingdom (2 Sam. 11; 12:1–24; 15; 1 Kings 14:8; 15:3–5).

David also died at age seventy, which was not very old during those days (2 Sam. 5:4).

The Bible says,

> "If we sin willfully after we have received the knowledge of the truth, there remains no more sacrifice for sins, but there is only a fearful expectation of judgment and fiery punishment. They who broke Moses' law died without mercy under two or three witnesses. How much sorer punishment for people who have trodden underfoot the Son of God, and have counted the blood of his covenant, wherewith he was sanctified, an unholy thing, and did it despite the Spirit of grace? It is a fearful thing to fall into the hands of the living

God." (Heb. 10:26–31; Exod. 20:18; 19; Deut. 5:23–26; Mic. 2:1; Ps. 19:12–14)

Remember the people in Moses's time begged to hear Moses, because if God himself had spoken to them, they would have surely died (Exod. 20:18–19; Deut. 5:23–26). God sent Ezekiel to warn the people, but God told him that the people will not listen to him because they would not listen to God (Ezek. 3:4–21). The Holy Scripture says that God's voice shook the earth in the Old Testament, but during these last and evil days, he will shake heaven and earth. Therefore, we must serve God with reverence and godly fear, for our God is a consuming fire and a jealous God, whose name is Jealous (Deut. 4:24; Exod. 34:14; Heb. 12:26–29).

If you do not repent, the wages of sin is still death (Rom. 1:18–32; 6:23; 2 Thess. 2:10–15; 8:13–14; 1 Kings 13:11–24; 1 Cor. 11:23–30; Ezek. 7:13; 18:4; 33:11, 19–20; Deut. 30:19–20; Job 20:11; 24:19; 36:5–13; Ps. 1:5–6; Prov. 19:5, 9; 21:16; 27:20; 30:15, 16; Isa. 5:14; 13:9; Josh. 7:1–13; 1 Chron. 10:13–14; Rev. 2:23; Matt. 18:11–14; Lam. 3:31–33; 1 Tim. 2:4; 2 Pet. 3:9; Luke 13:1–5).

REFUSING TO BELIEVE THAT REBELLIOUS PEOPLE REAP DEATH, DESTRUCTION, & HELL

God reminds us of him destroying the entire world except eight people in the days of Noah, because everyone refused to live holy and sanctified except Noah's family. God also reminds us of how he destroyed the cities of Sodom and Gomorrah at another time in history and that when he returns this time, one spouse will be taken to heaven and the other left behind (Luke 17:20–37; 2 Tim. 3:1–7). Jesus says if a person could come back from hell to tell the world how bad hell is, some people still would not believe that they also can be cast into hell. That scripture also says that if people did not believe Moses and the prophets, some people nowadays will not believe that they can go to hell even if someone returned from hell to warn them (Luke 16:19–31; Acts 13:41). That is true, because people did not and do not believe after Christ came from heaven to warn the people of the earth while simultaneously saving the souls of people, healing them, and delivering them. Christ asked one man, how can he believe heavenly things while not believing what Christ said about earthly things (John 3:12–13). In terms of suffering for sins, sometimes seeing is not believing (Jer. 3:8).

To people who go on in sin, God says, "Because they do not regard the works of the Lord, nor the operation of his hands, he shall destroy them and not build them up" (Ps. 28:4-5).

People who trust in their own hearts are fools (Prov. 28:26; Isa. 65:2). The Lord says,

> "The fool has said in their heart, there is no God. They are corrupt; they have done abominable works; there is none who does good. The Lord looked down from heaven upon humans, to see if there are any who understand, who seek God. They are all gone back; they are all together become filthy; there is none who does good, no, not one. Do the workers of sin have any knowledge? They eat up my people like they eat bread. They have not called upon God." (Ps. 14:1-4; 53:1-4; Rom. 3:10-18).

"For thus says the high and lofty One who inhabits eternity, whose name is Holy, I dwell in the high and holy place with people who are of a contrite and humble spirit" (Isa. 57:15). The Lord is near unto people who are of a broken heart toward him and he saves people who are of a contrite spirit (Ps. 34:18). The sacrifice that God wants from us is a broken spirit and a broken and contrite heart, and people who tremble at his Word. As a result, and a reward, God will revive the spirit and heart of people with a contrite heart toward him, but worldly sorrow causes death (Isa. 57:15; 66:1-2; Ezra 9:6; 2 Cor. 7:9-10; Ps. 34:15-18; 38:15-18; 51:17; 85:8; Ezek. 18:21-22).

The Bible says to the pure God will show himself pure, but to the sinful, he will show himself shrewd (2 Sam. 22:27; Ps. 18:26).

David said that God covered him in the womb and God caused him to trust in the Lord from the time God took him out of his mother's womb and laid him on her breast (Ps. 22:9-10; 71:6; 139:13). And Christ says that we must become as little children, humble, meek, and leaning on the Lord, if we are to be saved

(Matt. 18:1–6; 19:13–15). Trust in the Lord with all your heart and lean not unto your own understanding. In all your ways, acknowledge him, and he shall direct your paths. The Word of God is a light unto your paths (Ps. 119:105; Prov. 4:18; Jer. 29:11–13). Christ says that we must deny ourselves daily to be a good Christian (Luke 9:23–26). "Be not wise in your own eyes, fear the Lord, and depart from evil. It shall be health to your navel, and marrow to your bones" (Prov. 3:5–8; 2 Chron. 31:21; Num. 15:39–41). The heart and tongue of mankind must be of the Lord, but the ways of humans are right in their own eyes. Commit your works unto the Lord and he shall establish your thoughts. Everyone who is proud in heart is an abomination to the Lord and shall not go unpunished. By the fear of the Lord, mankind departs from evil, and when the ways of mankind please the Lord, he makes even their enemies to be at peace with them. A person's heart makes plans according to their ways, but God must direct your steps (Prov. 16:1–9). God will keep people in perfect peace, whose mind is stayed on him, because they trust in God (Isa. 26:3). "If you allow righteousness to go before you, your health shall spring forth speedily" (Isa. 58:8). People who depart from evil will be persecuted by sinners, so brace yourself and trust in the Lord (Isa. 59:15).

CHRIST DID SPEAK AGAINST HOMOSEXUALITY & UNGODLY POLITICS

Some people say Jesus himself did not speak on homosexuality, but he did because "In the beginning was the Word, the Word was with God, and the Word was God. The same was in the beginning with God, and the Word was made flesh, and dwelt among us" (John 1:1-3, 14; 1 John 5:6-8; Prov. 8:22-36; Job 27:11). Therefore, when authors in the Bible wrote scriptures, including the part about homosexuality being against God's will, Christ said it through them because he is the Word, and the Word was here from the beginning of the earth. Also, Christ himself said when he was in the form of a human, "In the beginning God made male and female, and a man should leave his father and mother and cleave unto his wife" (Matt. 19:4). He did not say that a man should cleave unto another man or a woman unto another woman.

Some people say Jesus himself did not speak on homosexuality, but he did because "In the beginning was the Word, the Word was with God, and the Word was God. The same was in the beginning

God speaks against homosexuality in the Old and New Testaments, and some of the Old Testament still applies to us.

The law of the Old Testament was until John the Baptist who paved the way for Christ (Matt. 3:1–3, 9, 11;13; John 1:15–17).

All that Jesus did not change when he walked on earth still applies, because Christ did not come to destroy the law but to fulfill it (Matt. 5:17–18; Luke 16:17). And Romans 13:8 says that when we love all people, we have fulfilled the law, including homosexuals. But homosexuals must love the Lord by obeying his Word, and Christ says that if we claim to love him, then we should obey his Word (John 14:15; Exod. 20:6; Lev. 26:3–6; Deut. 5:10; 13:4).

Some people also say that Christ did not discuss politics, but Christ did address politicians. He often called them hypocrites (Matt. 22:16–21). Politicians in the Bible included such parties as the Sadducees, Pharisees, Herodians, and lawyers (Luke 11:45–46, 52; Matt. 16:1–4; 23:13–15, 23, 27–33).

Jesus did say, "Render unto God the things that belong to God and unto Caesar the things that belong to Caesar" (Matt. 22:15–22). What this means in today's generation is that the law of the land does allow rights for almost anything in society that people want to do, but that does not mean that anti-God laws should be supported by Christians. Men who wrote the constitution of the United States, for example, owned slaves and limited women to very minimal rights, so the constitution is not perfect, and it should not be followed so closely that we neglect to do what God wants us to do. And when politicians, the media, celebrities, and hypocrite Christians say it is right for gays to marry, they are stealing a spiritual patent, trademark, and copyright from God and should be sued by the church for stealing what the church put in place from the beginning of time (John 1:1–2, 14). Also in the New Testament, certain people persecuted the apostles for teaching the Word of God that was contrary to the decrees of Caesar (Acts 17:6–7).

Speaking of the beginning of time, God did not want his people under a political system like other nations (2 Kings 17:15; 1

Chron. 1:43–54). He rebuked his people when they desired a king instead of allowing him to be their One and only King (1 Sam. 8:1–7, 19–20; Hosea 8:4). Christ should be the King of all Christians, but when they support homosexuality, they are personally dethroning King Jesus. When God's people desired a political king like we desire political presidents, most of those kings caused the people to practice sin like anti-God nations did. So the prophets such as Isaiah, Jeremiah, Ezekiel, and Daniel spoke against those kings and other people who claimed to be God-loving and God-fearing people while they emulated the heathens of the world and while they disobeyed the prophets of God, even while the prophets spoke of the first and second coming of Christ (Dan. 9; Isa. 7:14; 8:8; 9:6; 11:1; 52:13–15; 53; Acts 28:23).

And in the New Testament, the Apostle Paul went around the world speaking out against hypocritical churches and governments. "Blessed are they who hunger and thirst after righteousness, for they shall be filled" (Matt. 5:6; Ps. 42:1–3; Prov. 15:8–9).

Some people make themselves rich but have nothing, because they are empty, blind, miserable, and unsaved (Prov. 13:7; Rev. 3:15–22). God fills spiritually hungry people with good things but sends the rich away empty (Luke 1:53). Notice that the scripture did not say that the hungry were filled with food, but with good things, whatever their soul hungers and thirsts for. Sometimes we must seek God and not simply wait on him to show up—seek and you shall find (Luke 11:9–10; Matt. 11:28–30; Jer. 6:16). Sinners shall seek but not find and call upon God, but he will not always answer (Luke 6:25; Prov. 1:28–30).

Politics have always been addressed in the Bible. Here is more proof. Jesus told his disciples, "When they bring you unto the synagogues, authorities, rulers, magistrates, and powers, take no thought how or what thing you shall answer, or what you shall say, for the Holy Ghost shall teach you in the same hour what you ought to say" (Luke 12:11–12).

Every tongue shall confess, and every knee shall bow to Christ, now or when they are begging God to not send them to hell (Isa. 45:23; Rom. 14:11; Phil. 2:9–12). All Christians must *stand* with God and against homosexuality and gay marriage and the adoption of children by gay people. Gay marriages are not done in holy matrimony because they are against God. The Bible says that we must cry aloud like a trumpet against sin and spare not and tell people about their sins and transgressions against God. When we do not speak out, the nation acts as though they are righteous (Isa. 58:1–2; 2 Cor. 13:2, 10; Ps. 40:9). John the Baptist in the New Testament cried aloud while preaching repentance, sanctification, and the seeking of the kingdom of heaven first (Matt. 3:1–3; Mark 1:3–4; John 1:23). God does not use coward soldiers (Num. 32:6–12; Deut. 20:2–4, 8–9; Judg. 7:1–3).

We must be sanctified in the Lord in the presence of heathens (Ezek. 20:41). The Word of God is good to people when they first hear it, but bitter when it is time to stand for the truth (Matt. 13:1–23; Ps. 81:10–16; Jer. 15:15–21; Rev. 10:9–11).

We must not be afraid to speak of God in the presence of kings and other politicians (Ps. 119:46–47; Jude 1:3). Because God blesses us in the presence of enemies and nonbelievers, we must certainly stand for his Word and bless Christ openly (Ps. 31:19, 23; 1 Pet. 3:15).

To people who say they supported President Obama and any politician because they provided certain benefits for them, the Bible says, "The Lord is on my side, I will not fear. What can man do to me? The Lord is for me. Therefore, I shall see my desire on those who hate me. It is better to trust in the Lord than to put confidence in mankind or in politicians" (Ps. 56:4; 118:6–9). God says he gives us daily benefits (Ps. 68:19; 103:2; 106:5; 116:12). Josiah was the most righteous king in the Bible, second to King Jesus. He trusted in the Lord with all his heart, he held fast to the Lord, he did not depart from following the Lord, and he obeyed the Word of God. And God was with him, he prospered wherever he went, and he rebelled against a heathen king and did not serve that king (2 Kings 18:5-7; 23:19-25). Hallelujah. Hezekiah followed and trusted in the Lord, removed idolatry, obeyed the Lord's Word, rebelled against the king of Assyria, and did not serve him, and the Lord was with Hezekiah, and he prospered (2 Kings 18:1, 4-7).

Most people do not even consider God (Isa. 1:3; Job 34:27; Hosea 7:2). But God Almighty says that the Lord will come to execute judgment upon all people, and to remind all people who are ungodly of all their ungodly deeds and of all their hard speeches that they have made against the Lord. They are murmurers, complainers, and walk after their own lusts and they speak with admiration and respect of persons for personal advantage. Beloved, remember the words of the apostles of Jesus Christ when they said that there will be mockers in these last days who walk after their own ungodly lusts, but Christ will keep you from falling and present you faultless and blameless to God if you continue to live holy (Jude 1:14-25)—just as Christ did not lose any of the disciples that God gave him, except Judas, who was lost to fulfill prophesy (John 17:12). God Almighty says that he will see whose word will stand, his or politicians, false prophets and false preachers, hypocrite Christians, or blasphemers (Jer. 44:26-29). God's Word will not return to him void (Isa. 14:24; 46:9-1; 55:10- 11; Jer. 23:20; Ezek. 5:13; 6:9-10; 7:13; 12:21-28; 22:14; 24:13-14; Dan. 9:12-14; Matt. 24:32-44; 2 Pet. 3:6-14; 2 Kings 10:10).

BENEFITS OF MARRIAGE & WHAT THE MAGNA CARTA REALLY MEAN

Some gay couples desire to marry so they can have the same tax benefits, insurance benefits, and retirement benefits as heterosexuals who are married in holy matrimony. To not have benefits could be part of their punishment from God for being gay. What if a heterosexual boyfriend and girlfriend wanted benefits because they have dated for a long time? Or what about common-law marriage between a man and a woman? Should they receive the same benefits of heterosexual couples who are legally married? The answer is no.

According to the way the Constitution of the United States of America is written, gays probably do have the right to marry and make legal and medical decisions according to man's law. But the Founding Fathers probably still did not want this to happen, or they would have said so, and Christians should be the first people to embrace the fact that the Constitution, the British Magna Carta, and the law of any land is not the Holy Bible and they are the words of humans and not the Word of God (Mark 7:6–7; Isa. 29:13; Col. 2:22; Titus 1:14; 1 Thess. 2:13).

Politicians today are basing their decisions on what they think the Founding Fathers meant while neglecting to face the fact that the Founding Fathers were not God and could not foresee the future as God always has been able to foresee. Thus, politicians, lawmakers, and some citizens use the constitution to corrupt society, because there are many loopholes in the constitution, such as the right for almost anyone to own an assault weapon and a woman's right to kill an unborn baby, even after several months of developing in the mother's womb. Some humans also used the law of the land to justify the oppression of black people by white people long after slavery was abolished.

WE MUST SACRIFICE SIN LIKE CHRIST SACRIFICED PROSPERITY & HIS WHOLE LIFE

It is our reasonable service to obey Christ, considering he sacrificed his life by living a pitiful life, suffering persecution, and dying in our place. God commands us to present our bodies a living sacrifice, holy, acceptable unto God, which is your reasonable service and our duty (Rom. 12:1–2; Luke 17:7–10; Eccles. 12:13–14; Deut. 10:12– 14; Heb. 12:26–29).

Speaking of being a living sacrifice, God asked Abraham to kill his son as a sacrifice unto the Lord God Almighty just to see if he would do it. But just before Abraham killed his child, God stopped him because he saw that Abraham was faithful and loyal.

God is not asking you to kill your child, but if your child is gay, God is asking you to sacrifice your support of their gay lifestyle so you and hopefully they too will be a living sacrifice. If you cannot stand with God in this day and age by refusing to support your family members or friends in their homosexuality, you certainly would not have obeyed God if he had asked you to kill your child for God's sake.

David said, "Because your loving-kindness is better than life, my lips shall praise you. I will lift my hands in your name" (Ps. 63:1– 4). That scripture has several meanings, including dying and going to heaven, which is better than living on earth, but it also means that the reward of God's loving-kindness is better than living a sinful lifestyle, thus denying yourself. The Apostle Paul said that he was persuaded that neither life nor death could separate us from the love of God (Romans 8:38–39). How can life separate us from the love of God? The answer is that a sinful life can separate us from God although he still loves us, and a righteous life obviously will not separate us from God. The Bible clearly states that sin separates us from our God (Isa. 1:15; 59:1–2; 64:4–8; Ps. 107:17–22; Mal. 2:2).

GOD IS ASHAMED OF PEOPLE WHO DO NOT STAND FOR HIS WORD

God is not ashamed of any of us no matter what we have done, but if anyone in this adulterous and sinful generation is ashamed to live like Christ and according to the Bible, then God becomes ashamed of them (Mark 8:34–38; Matt. 10:32–33; 24:3–14; Job 27:8–23; 1 Thess. 2:2; 2 Tim. 1:12; James 1:8–27; Rev. 3:1–6).

Christ sanctified himself so we too can be sanctified through the truth (John 17:17–19; Isa. 29:23). But do not be ashamed to be sanctified, because God who sanctifies us is not ashamed to call sanctified people his very own (Heb. 2:11; 11:16). Sanctified simply means to be set apart for holy use and to live holy, for without holiness, no one can see God (Ps. 4:3–5; Heb. 12:14–15; Rom. 12:1–2; 2 Tim. 2:19–26).

Notice that those same scriptures say that we can fail the grace of God, so do not take grace for granted. And another scripture says, "Do not receive the grace of God in vain" (2 Cor. 6:1–10). We must not continue in sin even though we are under grace, and the price of sin is death (Rom. 6:1–11, 23; Jude 1:4). The Bible tells us to be strong in the grace that is in Christ Jesus and to not use grace as an excuse to be weak or to sin willfully (2 Tim. 2:1). God says, "Let us have grace," but we must still serve God acceptably with reverence and godly fear, because our God is a consuming fire and a jealous God (Heb. 12:28–29; Deut. 4:24). Christians must not even be ashamed to speak of God in the presence of kings and other politicians (Ps. 119:46–47; Jude 1:3; Acts 9:10–16). When people draw back from God after tasting the heavenly gift and the good Word of God and the powers of the new world to come in heaven, they crucify Christ over again and put him to an open shame (Heb. 6:1–6; Matt. 13:1–23).

Moses was favored by God more than most of us will ever be. Moses asked to see God's face, but God denied that request because if any human sees God's face, they will die (Exod. 33:17–23). God did allow Moses to see him from behind. Most people have not seen God in that way. And most Christians know that although Moses was highly favored by God, the Lord still did not allow Moses to enter the promised land due to disobedience (Num. 20:12; Deut. 3:23–28). Some people nowadays will not enter heaven because of disobedience (Heb. 3:7–19; 4:1). But what some Christians may not know is that even though Moses was a chosen vessel of God and a faithful servant of the Lord, God came very close to killing Moses at one point because of disobedience (Exod. 4:24–26). So although God is good, loving, kind, merciful, and full of grace, he can be very hard even on people who serve him in righteousness. The Bible says, "God is good, and does good. Teach me your statutes" (Ps. 119:68). But a lot of people including some Christians live by statutes that humans made, and that will result in pain, sorrow, sickness, death, and destruction (2 Kings 17:19; Ps. 28:4–5).

New Testament scripture says that if the righteous are scarcely saved, where will the sinner and the ungodly appear (1 Pet. 4:17–18; 1 Cor. 3:5–17; Prov. 14:32; Matt. 24:21–22)?

Christ says whosoever confesses him before humans, he will also confess that person before God, but if anyone denies Christ before mankind, Christ will deny them before God (Matt. 10:32–33). Great peace is with people who love God's Word, and nothing shall offend them (Ps. 119:165– 168). Blessed are they who are not offended in Christ (Matt. 11:6). This means that we cannot be ashamed to confess Christ openly against politicians, but we must also pray and stand for God's Word openly while speaking out against homosexuality and abortions (Ps. 119:46–47; Jude 1:3). The Apostle Paul was a vessel chosen to suffer great things for Christ's name sake before Jews, Gentiles, and kings who are also politicians (Acts 9:10–16).

Christ knows people who have only a little strength but still have not denied his name and his Word, and Christ says he sets an open door before them that no one can close, but Christ will say to hypocrites, "Depart from me you worker of iniquity" (Matt. 7:21–23; Mic. 3:11; Luke 13:24–27).

Even when people do a great work for the Lord, God may not perform his promises toward them until they do the work in holiness, in righteousness, and walk in his Word (2 Tim. 2:3–5; Rom. 11:29; 1 Kings 6:12).

PEOPLE WHO LIVE GODLY IN CHRIST JESUS SHALL SUFFER PERSECUTION

Christ says, "Do not fear any of the things you are about to suffer. The devil will even throw some of you in prison to test you. Be faithful until death, and I will give you the crown of life" (Rev. 2:10). Paul while in prison was faithful unto death, until he was murdered (2 Tim. 4:9–18). When you believe, you must also speak the truth (2 Cor. 4:13). If we suffer like Christ, we shall also reign with him, but if we deny him, he will also deny us (2 Tim. 2:12). Be not ashamed of the gospel of Jesus Christ but be partakers of the afflictions of the gospel according to the power of God (2 Tim. 1:8–9, 12). We must allow our light to shine for everyone to see, like a city on top of a hill (Matt. 5:14–16; Phil. 2:15). Paul said, "I am not ashamed of the gospel of Christ, for it is the power of God unto the saving of your soul. The "just" shall live by faith. For the wrath of God is revealed from heaven against all ungodliness and unrighteousness, and it is impossible to please God without faith (Rom. 1:16–18; Hab. 2:4; Gal. 3:11; Heb. 6:1–6; 10:38; 11:1, 6).

For we walk by faith, not by sight (2 Cor. 5:7). We should serve God without being afraid of any enemy (Luke 1:74; Lev. 26:6; Heb. 11:23–29; Ps. 119:134).

Business owners and managers such as those who have stood against homosexuality by not allowing gay couples to rent rooms in hotels, for example, or to not bake wedding cakes for gay couples have been sued. Christians who could not deny President Obama because of his anti-Christians beliefs are the same as the rich man in the Bible who could not obey Jesus when Jesus told him to give away all that he had (Matt. 19:16–22).

The store owner who was sued for refusing to bake a wedding cake for a gay couple closed their bakery instead of baking the cake.

That is a perfect example of denying yourself and standing with God. One of the members of the television show *Duck Dynasty* used Bible scripture to point out that homosexuals and all sinners are worthy of death. And that is exactly what the Bible says. He was suspended from the show for speaking God's Word, and the producers and many others thought that he would do what numerous other people have done, retract their statements and apologize. But he stood with God even if it meant that he would lose millions of dollars. The producers of the show soon reinstated him. All people who have been blessed by God to be in position of power can also force world lovers to back down, but they do not, because the world loves their own and are enemies of God (John 1:10–12; 15:18–19; James 4:4). Angus Jones, a then nineteen-year-old actor in the television show *Two and a Half Men*, stood with God by speaking out against the gay-themed show; he separated himself from the show, called himself a paid hypocrite, called the show filth, encouraged people not to watch it, and announced that no real Christian should work on the show. We all must stand with God no matter what we lose. They who find their worldly life shall lose their life, but they who lose their worldly life for Christ's sake shall find their life (Matt. 10:34–39; 1 John 5:12; 2 Tim. 2:9 – 13), because Christ lost his life, not only in obedience to God but also in support of us and in salvation of all our lives.

The Bible tells us that false prophets and false preachers shall continue to rise and show great signs and wonders, and if it were possible, they would deceive the very elect Christians (Matt. 24:24). Some false preachers and hypocrite preachers call evil things good and good things evil, are wise in their own eyes, and justify sinners, but they shall be punished (Isa. 5:20–25; 13:6–13; Rom. 3:4–8).

They who live godly in Christ Jesus shall suffer persecution like Christ did (2 Tim. 3:11–13; Ezek. 14:6–11; Heb. 3:7–13; Ps. 38:9–22; Jer. 15:15–21; John 16:20).

And if you are a Christian who is not persecuted occasionally, that means you are not living according to the Word of God and you are not standing for the Word of God. People who inherit eternal life in heaven with no pain, suffering, tears, or sickness shall enter heaven after plenty of tribulation on earth (Acts 14:21–22; Rev. 21:1–8; Luke 22:39–46). The Apostle Paul wrote,

> "We boast of you among the churches of God for your patience and faith in all your persecutions and tribulations that you endure, which is the manifest evidence of the righteous judgment of God, for which you also suffer. Since it is a righteous thing with God to repay with tribulation those who trouble you. And to give you who are troubled rest with us when the Lord Jesus is revealed from heaven with his mighty angels, in flaming fire taking vengeance on those who do not know God, and on those who do not obey the gospel of our Lord Jesus Christ. These shall be punished with everlasting destruction, when he comes in that day, to be glorified in his saints. Therefore we also pray for you that our God will count you worthy of this calling (2 Thess. 1:4–12).

Moses said, "Who is on the Lord's side come to me," not him to them (Exod. 32:26). Jesus says that when we are being persecuted for his sake, even to death for some people, and when family and friends betray us, we should continue to stand for the Word of God, and in "your patience you shall save your soul" (Luke 21:15-19; James 1:21).

Peter told Jesus that the apostles had left everything to follow him. Jesus replied, "There is no one who has left houses, brothers, sisters, father, mother, wife, children, or homeland for my sake, and the gospel's sake, who will not receive one hundred times more houses, brothers, sisters, mothers, children, and lands in this life, but with persecutions" (Mark 10:28-31; Job 1; 2:1-10; 13:15-16; 42; 1 Cor. 7:25-34; Luke 14:25-27, 33).

The scripture also says that after we are rewarded a hundred times on earth, we will receive eternal life in heaven (Mark 10:30).

A Miss America contestant was criticized for saying she did not believe in gay marriage. That was a trap question that should have never been asked. Everyone who lives godly in Christ Jesus shall suffer persecution, but sinners shall grow worse and worse, deceiving and being deceived by God and by mankind and devils (2 Tim. 3:1- 8, 11-13; Ezek. 14:6-11; 21:23-24; Heb. 3:7-13; Ps. 38:9-22; Jer. 15:15-21; John 16:20; 1 Thess. 2:10-15; 2 Thess. 2:9-12; Isa. 66:4; 1 Kings 22:23; Titus 1:16; Rom. 1:18-32).

POLITICAL & CHRONOLOGICAL EVENTS THAT LED TO LEGALIZING GAY MARRIAGES

The state of Vermont used civil unions to justify allowing gay couples to have benefits, but they did not call it marriage. On June 17, 2003, Canada announced that it was going to allow same-sex marriages, according to Prime Minister Jean Chretien. He called it a union between two people, or same-sex unions, deleting from their constitution "between man and woman." Before this, Belgium and the Netherlands were the only two countries to legalize gay marriage. Therefore, the attempt to get the entire world to accept homosexuality and gay marriages began in European nations and in nations that originated from Europe. Also, in Canada, in July of 2017, the first newborn baby was born to not have a gender designation on the birth certificate. A gay man was ordained bishop in 2003 in the Episcopal Church. Not only was this an abomination, but also it did not meet the spiritual and biblical standards and qualifications of a bishop (1 Tim. 3:1–7; Titus 1:5–11; 2 Tim. 3:1–5; Gal. 1:4).

Catholic priests have been found guilty of child molestation with boys. This occurred because some of the priests were gay before they became a priest. They used the priesthood to explain why they were not married to a woman and to have access to boys.

In early-to-mid-2013, a citizen in the Netherlands said that now that gays can legally marry in their country, the next fair thing to do would be to allow a man to have multiple wives at one time, which is polygamy. This should not be a surprise, because when you start something that you cannot finish, there is no telling what will be requested next. In December of 2013, a Utah judge ruled that to prosecute a man in that state for being married to multiple wives is a violation of that man's first amendment rights in the United States.

Just as one lie leads to another, one anti-God ruling and law leads to another. States that allow this live by the law that they made, not by the commandments that God made (2 Kings 17:19; Ps. 28:4–5). Some states legalized gay marriage to attract gay taxpayers who would move there for the freedom to marry and to adopt children.

Also in 2013, there was a push to legalize gay marriage in England and to use chapels and churches to perform gay marriages. Several Christian leaders opposed it, but the monarchy and royal family led by Queen Elizabeth did not take a stance against it, even though they confess and claim to be Christians.

On December 4, 2013, a Mississippi judge denied a lesbian couple a divorce because they were married in California and because gay marriage was not legal in Mississippi. If the judge had allowed it, then that would have set a precedent and enticed gay supporters to sue the state for the right to have gay marriages in the state. On December 9, 2013, a Colorado gay couple filed a lawsuit against a baker because he refused to bake their wedding cake due to it violating his religious beliefs. They who find their worldly life shall lose their life, but they who lose their worldly life for Christ's sake shall find their life (Matt. 10:34–39; 1 John 5:12; 2 Tim. 2:9 – 13). Also in Colorado, on January 10, 2015, a church refused to have a funeral of a lesbian woman whose family wanted a video to be played in memory of her that included scenes with her lesbian partner. The church was criticized for it, but they were right, and they stood not only for God but also with God and were persecuted for doing so, just as the Bible teaches us that when we live godly in Christ Jesus, we shall be persecuted (2 Tim. 3:11–12).

In 2018 in the United States, the female professional basketball league, the WNBA, announced that players will be required to wear game attire that celebrated gay pride, and television networks advertised it. But at least one female player rightfully opposed it and said that it was against her religion to support homosexuality.

On December 12, 2013, Australia struck down a law that legalized gay marriage and nullified all previous gay marriages.

Bill Clinton, former president of the United States, stood against homosexuality during his presidential terms. Years later, he said he regretted it. That could have been a public relations stunt on his part to fit in with the growing wicked society of the early 2000s, or he could have felt bad about offending gay people during his tenure as president but supporting them years later offended God Almighty (Matt. 11:6; Ps. 119:46–47, 165–168; Jude 1:3; Acts 9:10–16).

And yet again, if we are ashamed of Christ and his Word, then Christ becomes ashamed of us before his Father in heaven, even on judgment day (Mark 8:38; Matt. 10:32–33; 1 Thess. 2:2; 2 Tim. 1:12; Rev. 3:1–6).

On January 10, 2014, then Attorney General Eric Holder forced the state of Utah to recognize gay marriage that was on hold until the Supreme Court could decide. On that same date, police in New York were ordered to address transgender people by the sex that they claim to be, instead of what they were born as. In March of 2015, the state of Indiana gave in to pressure from the media and from sports industries when they amended their religious freedom law, because gays and their supporters said it would cause discrimination. It is not a coincidence that the pressure from anti-God people and businesspeople who promised to boycott the state was applied during the week of the college basketball championship, and the governor promised to change the law by the end of the week, which was just one day before the games began. The love of money is the root of all evil and causes many hurtful sorrows (1 Cor. 6:9–11; 1 Tim. 6:9–10; James 3:13–16; 2 Kings 5:15–27).

The fact that the mayor of South Bend, Indiana during this time was a gay man who was married to another man may have also played a part in getting the laws amended. This same gay mayor ended up seeking the nomination to run for president of the Unites States in the year 2020. This is what happens after President Obama became the first president to support gay marriage and gays adopting children, and some Christians wrongfully support it.

The state of Arkansas passed a similar bill that same week, and their governor too began to back out of the state's stance against homosexuality and their support of God. In David's last words, he said, "They who rule over mankind must be 'just,' and 'rule' in the 'fear' of God" (2 Sam. 23:2–3; Neh. 7:1–2). That pertains to preachers, law officials, politicians, and all leaders and authoritative figures (Ps. 72:1–2; 75:2; 54:3; Deut. 17:18–20; 32:12).

David knew to write that because he suffered greatly for his sins (1 Kings 14:8; 15:1–5; 2 Sam. 11; 12:1–24; 15).

The Bible also says regarding preachers, "Let the elders including ministers who rule well be counted worthy of double honor, especially they who labor in the Word and doctrine" (1 Tim. 5:17).

The Rev. Al Sharpton said during a radio commercial that he

is a minister and that he is telling everyone that it is right for gays to marry and that the people of Maryland should vote to legalize gay marriage. That is extremely hypocritical and blasphemous. On August 24, 2013, Al Sharpton was at the commemoration of the honorable fiftieth anniversary of the March on Washington where he quoted the Bible in the same sentence that he supported gay marriage. But the Bible says that blessings and cursing should not come out of the same mouth (James 3:10). Just as water fountains do not produce fresh water and saltwater, wise people with knowledge should show with good conversation their works with meekness of wisdom, without envying and strife, and they do not lie against the truth. Otherwise, that wisdom does not come from heaven, but from earth and from the devil, but wisdom from heaven is first pure and without hypocrisy (James 3:8–18).

On August 28, 2013, Dr. Bernice King, the daughter of the late great Dr. Martin Luther King Jr., made an eloquent and very articulate speech at the celebration of the fiftieth anniversary of the March on Washington DC. She mentioned a list of things in which minorities in America are discriminated against, and she said that people should not be discriminated against because of sexual orientation. Some preachers and Christians say things like that while not believing in homosexuality, but they are mainly stating that gays should have equal rights. That is true but not in terms of gay marriage and gays having the right to adopt children. Gays should not be beaten, battered, harassed, bullied, or prevented from having employment, specifically when the place of employment is not charged with setting the standard for children and young people, and that is not Christian-based or faith-based.

Bernice King is a Christian minister, but no minister or Christian should speak in support of gay relationships at all. If Bernice King, Al Sharpton, any preacher, or any Christian opposes homosexuality but still think that gays should have the equality of marriage and the right to adopt children, they must understand that God could be punishing gays by not allowing them to have equality in certain other areas of society, just as all sinners are punished by God in one way or another, and that gays should still be ashamed to proudly pronounce that they are gay. The Bible teaches us to be ashamed of sin, especially immoral sin (2 Tim. 3:1–5; Ezra 9:6; Jer. 31:19; Rev. 16:15), such as losing one's virginity before marriage, having children out of wedlock, committing rape, child molestation, adultery, and homosexuality. Should societies around the world demand that we accept and support people who commit those acts too? Those are sins, just as homosexuality is a sin, and people should be ashamed of all those sins too. But to be openly proud to be gay and gays who marry each other and adopt children are anti-God.

In 2003, it was reported that a city in New York planned to open a gay public high school. In December 2003, a judge in Iowa gave a lesbian couple a divorce who were married in Vermont. He did it by signing the papers without knowing that they were gay. When he realized what he had done, he refused to change it, even though he did not believe in it. The judge should have stood for righteousness and ruled in the fear of God (Eph. 6:13; 2 Sam. 23:3; Neh. 5:15; Ps. 19:9).

On May 15, 2004, ABC News in the United States showed a lesbian couple receiving sperm from a gay male couple to have children for both households! On February 24, 2004, Pres. George W. Bush called for a constitutional amendment making it unconstitutional for gays to marry. But on July 14, 2004, the US Senate refused to vote on the issue. They said Bush did that to increase his chances of getting reelected. Maybe so, but they should have voted against homosexual marriage, for God's sake. Republicans in the United States usually support the Bible and stand against homosexuality more than Democrats do, and hopefully many of those Republicans live holy, God-fearing, sanctified lives and do not oppress poor people and minorities. But some of those Republicans only speak against homosexuality because their political party stands against it and not because they truly oppose homosexuality. It is still very pleasing to God when Republicans stand against homosexuality and abortions, and God is angry with Democrats and any person who supports or believes in homosexuality and abortions. God says he is angry with wicked people every day, until they repent, turn from those sins, and stand against those sins (Ps. 5:4–7; 7:11; 11:5–7; 34:16; Isa. 5:20–25; 13:6–13).

Black people must realize and understand that times change, and parties change. The Democrat Party is the party that supported slavery and starting the Civil War. Abraham Lincoln was a Republican when he freed black slaves. South Carolina and Mississippi were the first two states to rebel and leave the United States, and they were mostly Democrats. The president of the Confederacy was a Mississippian and a Democrat. Democrats were the party of the Ku Klux Klan and other Jim Crow, oppressive, terrorizing, and genocidal practices, and policies. When Republicans failed to support black people during the Great Flood of 1927 in the Mississippi Delta and allowed armed white men to force black people at gunpoint to work on the levee until it broke and killed the black men, that is when black people started supporting Democrats. But now times and parties have changed again, and Democrats are now a lot more anti – God, blasphemous, hypocritical, evil, wicked than the Republican Party.

The mayor of San Francisco spoke out against President Bush and issued marriage licenses to gay people even though it was illegal in California. On February 13, 2004, Massachusetts and California performed marriage ceremonies illegally and admitted that the gay couples did not have the rights of real and heterosexual married couples. On May 17, 2004, gay marriage was legalized in Massachusetts, but churches fought for a voter ratification. This issue was a big reason that President Bush was reelected, but he never made gay marriage illegal, because he got what he wanted, to be reelected; then he turned his back on God. That was a political move and a lie on Bush's part.

During the presidential election of 2004, several states voted to ban gay marriage. On September 6, 2005, the California State Legislature approved a bill allowing gays and lesbians to wed. On September 29, 2005, Gov. Arnold Schwarzenegger vetoed the bill. God bless him for doing so. Years later, the voters of California voted to not allow gays and lesbians to marry, but a judge, who some say was gay, overturned the people's choice of not approving gay marriage. In several states of the United States, the citizens of those states voted to keep marriage between one man and one woman, but all it took was one perverted, evil, and anti-God judge to overturn the decisions of the citizens of the respective states.

The nation of France made gay marriage legal in 2013 after following the lead of several other nations. On April 29, 2013, a gay professional basketball player became the first openly gay athlete. President Obama called the gay player and congratulated him. The gay basketball player was probably proud to receive a phone call from the president of the United States, but God called him too, and in terms of homosexuality, he did not answer God as he answered for a man who happened to be a president. We all must answer God one day, even if it is a death call. And no one can see God without holiness (Heb. 12:14–15; Rom. 12:1–2; 2 Tim. 2:15). "Let us cleanse ourselves from all filthiness of the flesh and spirit, perfecting holiness in the fear of God" (2 Cor. 7:1).

President Obama also spoke on behalf of the first openly gay professional football player. The television network ESPN and other networks at that time were also anti-God because they embraced and highlighted repeatedly the gay football player kissing in the mouth his boyfriend after he was finally drafted into professional football. But just about one week before that, ESPN did not embrace or highlight, but they edited and cut out the words of the most valuable player of the NBA, Kevin Durant, when he said that he would first like to thank God who changed his life and who caused him to know what life is about and that basketball is only a platform.

Muslims and other certain religions do not accept or support homosexuality nearly as much as so-called Christians. Some people who go by the name of God have actually done worse things than people who do not claim to be Christians (Jer. 2:32–33; 5:28–31; 2 Chron. 28:1–4; 33:9; Matt. 5:19; 23:15; 2 Kings 21:10–12; Lam. 4:6; Ezek. 16:27, 44–63; 23:1–11, 37–39; Judg. 19:11–30; 20:1–14; 1 Cor. 5:1–6, 9–13; 1 Tim. 5:8; Hosea 10:12–15; Rev. 2:20).

PEOPLE IN THE SOUTHERN PART OF THE USA STAND AGAINST HOMOSEXUALITY THE MOST

The southern region of the United States is called the Bible Belt because they support the Holy Bible more than any other region in the United States. The South also has a history of slavery and oppression, and southern Christians must be careful not to be hypocrites by standing against homosexuality and abortions while being guilty of oppression, prejudice, discrimination, respect of persons, and racism. But critics who do not live by the Bible should not be quick to point out the dark past and occasional present-day incidents of the South and the Bible Belt if the critics themselves are living in darkness in other ways. If we say we have fellowship with Christ but walk in darkness, we lie. But if we walk in the light of Christ, we have fellowship with one another, regardless of race or ethnic background (1 John 1:5–10; John 1:1–14; 8:2–12).

Christ made people from all nations one blood and one spiritual race (1 John 2:2–4; Acts 17:26; Heb. 2:9; Rom. 5:6–9; 8:32; Isa.

53).

If you say you fear God and obey his voice but still walk in darkness, hatred, and hypocrisy, then you do not truly trust in the Lord and you do not truly rely on him or obey him (Isa. 50:10; 2 Kings 17:20–41). The beginning of wisdom is to fear God (Ps. 111:10). Christ lived life on earth more like black people than any other race in the world; therefore middle-class, upper-class, and rich people should be extremely careful not to become arrogant or to become prejudice, oppressing, and discriminating anti-Christ people themselves (Isa. 53:3–4, 7; Gen. 15:13; 2 Cor. 8:9; Phil. 4:19; Lev. 12:6–8; Luke 2:21–24; Rom. 15:1–3; Dan. 7:9–10; Rev. 1:13–15).

CRUCIFIXION OF CHRIST BY PRESIDENT OBAMA & HYPOCRITE CHRISTIANS

During his campaign for reelection, Pres. Barack Obama of the United States made history by becoming the first American president to openly support gay marriage. Some people said that if he had not supported homosexuality and abortions, he would have lost the election. But the Bible says, "What does a person profit if they gain the whole world [or a presidential election] and lose their soul to hell's fire" (Mark 8:36–38). In 2010, President Obama met in the Oval Office with leaders of the military and told them to support homosexuality in the military or resign. After he was reelected, he asked the Supreme Court to overrule the voter's decision by disregarding their votes and to make gay marriage legal. He also stated that Boy Scouts of America should change their policies of not accepting gay people in their organization. Later in 2013, Boy Scouts of America mandated that homosexuals can openly be members of their organization. As a result, churches in the southern part of the United States severed ties with Boy Scouts of America, and rightfully so.

The people of California fought hard to keep marriage between one man and one woman. The US Supreme Court heard the case and a case on whether the Defense of Marriage Act was unconstitutional. During this time, they crucified Christ again not only because many supporters of homosexuality confess Christ but also because the Supreme Court heard those cases during resurrection week in 2013, and they began the hearing on the exact day of Christ's trial more than two thousand years earlier. And the Supreme Court ended their arguments on the exact anniversary that Jesus was hung on the cross and laid in the tomb. Their arguments were concluded. As the Bible puts it, Christians who supported the Supreme Court's decision helped to crucify Christ afresh and put Christ to an open shame (Heb. 6:6). God says that he has sanctified his great name and that he is to be sanctified in us in the eyes of the heathen (Ezek. 20:41; 28:25; 36:23).

The Supreme Court and Pres. Barack Obama played the role of the Roman government in Israel when Christ lived on earth, and many Christians played the role of the Jews who told the Romans to go ahead and crucify Christ. This is exactly how the US Supreme Court crucified Jesus again. They started arguments in support of gay marriage on Tuesday, March 26, 2013—the exact anniversary that Jesus was betrayed by Judas, arrested, beaten, mocked, spat on, falsely accused, denied by Peter, and tried in court. That is also the exact day that the Supreme Court started hearing arguments against the Word of God and in support of homosexual marriage.

When the Supreme Court ended their first day of arguments, they locked Jesus up until the next day while persecuting him in their hearts, in written language, and in their actions. There were also Christians that night in various parts of the world who denied Christ like Peter did more than two thousand years ago because they started the day against gay marriage, and that night, they changed their minds and denied Christ. When the Supreme Court opened their doors on Wednesday, March 27, 2013, that was the exact anniversary that Jesus was placed on the cross more than two thousand years earlier. On that day, the Supreme Court put Christ on the cross afresh while they argued their last day of arguments in defense of gay marriage, crucifying Jesus again, on the anniversary of his crucifixion and in the middle of the Christian celebrated Holy Week, Passion Week, resurrection week, Passover week, and what most people in error call Easter week. This was a deliberate and purposeful act of Satan, who used Pres. Barack Obama and the Supreme Court to crucify Christ again by hearing the arguments in support of gay marriage in the middle of the week that the world celebrated the death and resurrection of our Lord and Savior Jesus Christ. They crucified Christ again by disregarding his Word and the Bible (Heb. 6:6). Christians who supported homosexuality crucified Christ again like the Romans and Jews crucified Christ in the past.

In this present time, the US Supreme Court is the same as the Romans in the Bible, and Christians who support homosexuality are the same as the Jews who chose a criminal instead of choosing Christ and some Christians chose President Obama instead of Christ. When the Supreme Court heard closing arguments on March 27, 2013, that was the exact anniversary that Christ carried his cross to the hill, was nailed to the cross, died, pierced in the side with a spear, and was taken off the cross and put in the tomb. The Bible says Jesus's body could not stay on the cross all night, based on God's law. Therefore, Christ's dead body was not put in the tomb on Good Friday, but on a Wednesday (Dan. 9:26–27; Deut. 21:22 – 23; John 19:25 – 37; Gal. 3:13), just as the Supreme Court symbolically put him in the tomb afresh on Wednesday, March 27, 2013, with Resurrection Day, also erroneously called Easter, being the following Sunday. It was impossible for Christ to stay in the grave three days and three nights if he was buried on Friday. The Romans guarded the grave three days, and Mary Magdalene went to the grave Sunday morning while it was still dark and Jesus had already risen and exited the tomb on what we now call Saturday night. That is three days. Christ was buried on a Wednesday, just as more than two thousand years later in 2013 the Supreme Court heard the final arguments on Wednesday in support of gay marriage.

During Easter week 2013, Satan laughed at Christians who believe it is all right for gays to marry. Those same Christians say they know Christ, but Satan knows Christ too. The difference is that Satan trembles at the name of Christ, but most people do not (James 2:19; Mark 3:9–12). Satan is more powerful than most humans, but humans should also fear God just as Satan fears God and knows that he will spend eternity in hell (Eph. 6:11–17; Isa. 66:1–2). After hearing the Apostle Paul, Felix trembled, but he told Paul that he would talk to him later (Acts 24:25–26). We must walk in the fear of God and in the comfort of the Holy Ghost (Acts 9:31). Some Christians confess Jesus Christ and that they know him, but in works, they deny him, being abominable, disobedient, and reprobate (Rom. 1:18–32; 2 Thess. 2:10–15; 8:13–14; 1 Pet. 2:6–8; 2 Tim. 3:1–8; Titus 1:16; Ps. 81:10–12, 15).

On June 26, 2013, the US Supreme Court returned with its answer and legalized gay marriage in the state of California and struck down the Defense of Marriage Act, making it unconstitutional. This means gays had the right to federal benefits including the same tax benefits as heterosexual couples in states where gay marriages were legal. Obama even called the people who rallied outside of the Supreme Court to congratulate them.

On June 26, 2015, the Supreme Court voted 5 to 4 to legalize gay marriage in all fifty states in the United States. President Obama openly supported their decision, and later that day, he delivered the eulogy of a pastor who was also a congressman who was shot to death in a South Carolina church along with eight others by a white supremacist. Pres. Barack Obama should not have been allowed in the pulpit in the first place because he was an anti-Christian, a devil, a blasphemer, and a hypocrite. He certainly should not have been allowed to deliver the eulogy after praising the legalization of gay marriage just hours before the eulogy. A lot of black people forgot God to support a black president, because of his race. The clergy at the funeral should have told Barack Obama to have a seat in the sanctuary and learn the truth of God from them. This was a bad reflection on the church and could have indicated that those ministers were not true servants of Christ because they allowed President Obama to defile God's holy altar when they allowed him to speak, and he hypocritically led the song "Amazing Grace."

The Bible says blessings and curses should not come out of the same mouth. But Obama cursed God when he verbally supported the legalization of gay marriage, and he hypocritically tried to bless the family of that poor pastor who was killed while simultaneously attempting to bless all the people at the funeral. It was the greatest display of hypocrisy and evil that America had seen in a long time. And the black preachers present that day allowed and supported it.

Also, in 2015, after the national legalization of gay marriage in the United States, several chancery clerks in the state of Mississippi and around the nation resigned from their positions instead of signing and issuing marriage licenses to gay couples. That is called carrying your cross, accepting persecution that God's true servants shall suffer, and standing for the truth (2 Tim. 3:11–12; Ps. 38:9–22). A woman in the state of Kentucky took it even further when she refused to resign, but she instead went to jail for days and returned to work while still refusing to issue marriage licenses to gay people. Although her deputies signed and issued the licenses, the clerk stood with God Almighty, in Christ's name, and against the evil law of the land.

BIDEN'S BLASPHEMOUS, HYPOCRITICAL & ANTI-GOD COMMENTS

Barack Obama's Vice President, Joe Biden, announced that he thought gays should have the right to marry, and he made that statement while Barack Obama was still refusing to support homosexual marriage. Many people felt that Joe Biden was insubordinate when he openly supported gay marriage while Obama was still opposing gay marriage. Mr. Obama later said that Joe Biden apologized to him for making the comments. Joe Biden made additional extremely evil comments when he said, "I do not think that most Americans want to live by a Bible that was written more than two thousand years ago." If any Christian does not understand that they should not support such anti-God, evil, hypocritical, and blasphemous people like Joe Biden and Barack Obama, then those Christians are also anti-God and blasphemous.

IT IS IMPOSSIBLE FOR REAL CHRISTIANS TO SUPPORT HOMOSEXUALITY

If Christians do not understand that gays cannot marry according to God, or if they understand and still voted for Barack Obama, they are deceived, or they are extremely neglectful and blasphemous toward God. The Bible says that it is impossible to deceive the elect Christians (Matt. 24:24). Great peace is with people who love God's Word, and nothing shall offend them (Ps. 119:165–168). We should all want to be elect saints. Jesus says that his people know his voice and will not follow another and that they will in fact run away from anything that is anti-Christian (John 10:1–5; Eph. 5:1–2). At one time, when it looked like God did not have a lot of followers who stood for the Word, God said, "I have seven thousand people in this place who have not bowed down to an idol god, neither have they kissed an idol's face" (1 Kings 18:26–32; 19:15–18; Rom. 11:1–5; 1 Kings 18:26–32; Deut. 5:9).

The same applies toward all people who did not vote for Barack Obama, especially black people who did not support President Obama and other evil and perverted politicians. They did not idolize Barack Obama because he was black like them.

The Bible says that people who walk spiritually upright shall be saved, but they who are perverse shall fall at once (Prov. 28:18). Perverse people despise and hate God, whether they realize it or not, and attempt to pervert the gospel of Jesus Christ, and they are cursed by God for doing so (Prov. 14:2; Gal. 1:6–9). Those same scriptures tell us that even if an angel tells you something contrary to what is in the Bible, do not believe the angel either. Christians are to be blameless and harmless children of God, without rebuke, shining like a light in the world, in the midst of a crooked and perverted nation (Phil. 2:15; Ezek. 14:22–23; Deut. 32:4–5).

God is perfect, right, just, and full of truth and he has never sinned or lied (Deut. 32:4; 2 Chron. 19:6–10; Ps. 18:30).

And God's Son Jesus Christ was tempted in every way that we are tempted, but he still did not sin (Heb. 4:15). However, homosexuals, their supporters, and people who do not stand against homosexuality are corrupted, are not the children of God, and are part of a perverted and crooked generation (Deut. 32:5). We are the children of God only when we obey him and when we are holy, sanctified, and separate from the world (Acts 5:32; Luke 11:13; John 14:13–18, 26–27; Phil. 2:15; 1 Pet. 1:13–17; Rom. 8:1, 5–14; 2 Cor. 6:17–18; Deut. 32:4–5).

THE CREATOR OF ALL THINGS DID NOT CREATE ANYONE GAY

Bisexuality is also homosexuality—there is no middle ground, just as there is no middle ground between heaven and hell. God made male and female, husband and wife, Adam and Eve, not Adam and Steve (Gen. 1:27; 2:24; Matt. 19:4). In the beginning, before God made Eve, God said that it was not good for man to be alone, so he made a woman for Adam, not another man (Gen. 2:18). God made man in his own image, not in the image of a perverted man or perverted woman (Gen. 1:26–27; 5:3; 9:6; Isa. 43:7, 20–22; 1 Cor. 11:7; 15:47–55; Phil. 2:6–11; James 3:9).

In marriage, there is man and wife, not man and man, nor woman and woman. On judgment day, we shall see God like he is, and we shall be like him (Phil. 3:17–21; 1 John 3:2; Ps. 17:14–15).

But we cannot be like him in heaven if we do not strive to be like him on earth. The Bible says that we must live godly in this present world too (Titus 2:11–15). Remember, the Lord's Prayer says, "Let there be done on earth as it is in heaven" (Matt. 6:10). When we see God like he is, and when we become like him in heaven, he and we will not be gay, bisexual, or a lesbian; a drunkard, drug dealer, drug addict, fornicator, thief, adulterer, child molester, idolater, or a participant in pornography; or one who dresses in a sexually revealing way (1 Cor. 6:9–11; 1 Tim.

6:9–10; 2 Kings 5:15–27).

No matter what happens, God is always right (Ezek. 18:19–32; 2 Thess. 1:4–12). We must always confess and admit that God is right and that we are wrong, just as homosexuality is a wrong decision and a wrong influence and not the way God made a person (Exod. 9:27; Hosea 14:9; Judg. 16).

One man in the Bible admitted his wrong and asked God for mercy, but another man admitted his wrong and still suffered and died for his sins before God accepted him into heaven (Luke 18:9–14; 23:39–46). God is right in all his judgments and actions, but some people would rather suffer, die, and go to hell before they accept that God is always right (Rev. 16:5–11; 1 Pet. 2:23; Jer. 11:20; Ps. 67:4; 96:10; 119:75–77; Dan. 9:14).

CHRISTIANS WHO SUPPORT GAYS ARE SELF-RIGHTEOUS & ANTICHRIST

We must not obey God's Word with partiality (1 Tim. 5:20–21). The Bible tells us that we cannot live by bread, money, civil rights, or politics alone but by every Word of God (Luke 4:4; Exod. 24:7). Jesus came unto his own people, and his own people did not receive him (John 1:10–14; Acts 13:26–31; Luke 24:44–49).

The same applies today when Christians do not openly oppose gay marriage and gay relationships; they reject Christ to support a human. Some Christians have a form of godliness but deny the power of God (2 Tim. 3:5). The Lord says, "If anyone is ignorant, let them be ignorant" (1 Cor. 14:38). They have a desire and zeal for God, but not according to knowledge. "For they are ignorant of God's righteousness, and going about to establish their own righteousness, have not submitted themselves unto the righteousness of God" (Rom. 10:2–3; Ps. 81:15).

Some Christians are ever learning but unable to come to the knowledge of the truth, having only a form of godliness, and they are not filled with the Spirit of God, nor do they live holy and sanctified lives (2 Tim. 3:1–7; 2 Pet. 3:14–18).

They live by rules that they made (2 Kings 17:19; Ps. 28:4–

5). They make mention of God, but not in truth, nor in righteousness (Isa. 48:1). They are crooked and perverted (Deut. 32:4–5). They speak evil of things they do not understand and shall utterly perish in their own corruption (2 Pet. 2:12–15; 1 Pet. 4:1–5). Some people profess and confess that they know God, but in works, they deny him, being abominable, disobedient, and reprobate unto every good work (Rom. 1:18–32; 2 Thess. 2:10–15; 8:13–14; 1 Pet. 2:6–8; 2 Tim. 3:1–8; Titus 1:16; Ps. 81:10–12, 15).

Awake to righteousness and sin not, for some do not know God as well as they think, even after seeing the works of God, because they are hard-hearted, so they shall not enter heaven (1 Cor. 15:34; Gal. 4:8–9; Heb. 3:7–12).

The law of the Lord is perfect, converting the soul and making wise the simpleminded. God's Word should enlighten our eyes and rejoice our heart. And the fear of the Lord should be desired more than gold, because God's Word warns us, and taking heed to his warnings gives us a long, good, protected, directed, and corrected life by the Lord (Ps. 19:7–14; 1 Cor. 10:5–8; Heb. 3:7–19; 4:1–2).

Christians who verbally support homosexuality should live by the scripture that says, "The opening of my lips shall be right things. For my mouth shall speak truth, and wickedness is an abomination to my lips. All the words of my mouth are in righteousness. There is nothing perverse in them" (Prov. 8:5–8).

God will not beg a person to love and embrace his Word, but he sometimes forces people to obey it while punishing them for their sins and when he calls them to do a service for him. However, many are called but few are chosen by God (Matt. 8:11–12; 20:16; 22:14).

CHRIST'S WORD IS LIKE A SWORD AND A FIRE

Christ says, "If your hand, foot, or eyes causes you to sin, spiritually but not literally cut them off, because it is better to live a life without hands, feet, and eyes than to have your whole body cast into hell" (Matt. 18:8–9). The same applies to your sex organs—spiritually but not literally cut them off before you allow them to get you thrown into hell's fire, whether it is heterosexual sex or homosexual sex, or your acceptance or support of it (Matt. 19:2–12; Rev. 14:1– 5). We must not love our family and friends to death in their sins and substance abuse, we must not enable them in sins and crimes, and we must not support them in sins and crimes. The Word of God also says, "If anyone comes to Christ and deny not their father, mother, wife, children, brothers, and sisters, yes, and their own life also, they cannot be Christ's servant. What profits a person to gain the whole world and lose their soul, and what will they give in exchange for their soul" (Mark 8:36–37; Luke 12:4–5; James 1:8–27; Job 27:8– 23; 1 Cor. 7:25–34)?

Whosoever does not bear their own cross and pursue Christ cannot be his servant (Luke 14:26–27; Deut. 33:9). This is to say that we are not to hate the sinner but hate the sin and not allow it in your home, your heart, nor in your conversation in support of it. Hatred of people stirs up strife, but love causes us to forgive sinners (Prov. 10:12; James 5:19–20).

If you are in favor of gay relationships, you must forsake that thought process and those actions immediately or you cannot be God's disciple. But when you do forsake those thoughts and actions, and when you help people who are in need and who are imprisoned, you shall be blessed in this present time and inherit everlasting life in the world to come, which is heaven (Luke 18:29–30; Matt. 19:29; Heb. 10:34).

Levi did not spare his mother, father, brother, sister, or his own children but he observed and guarded God's Word (Deut. 33:9). The child prophet Samuel was asked by his mentor the older prophet Eli to tell him the truth about what God revealed to him. Samuel told him that his house and his sons will be greatly punished for their sins, and Eli accepted God's punishment and said, "Let the Lord do what seems good to him" (1 Sam. 3:11–18).

Hezekiah also accepted God's Word and punishment and said, "God's word is good" (2 Kings 20:1–7, 14–19). One man told Christ that he would follow and serve him, but that Christ first had to allow him to go bury his dead father. Jesus told him that if anyone labors in his name and looks back, they are not fit for the kingdom of God (Luke 9:62). This also pertains to Christians who did not support gay relationships but later changed their minds. Christ does not require us to not attend the funerals of loved ones. He used that example to illustrate to us how serious he is about people confessing his name while setting a poor example as a Christian. But if God does require us to miss a funeral to do his work, it would be in our best interest to obey God.

You probably have heard of Jesus being the Prince of Peace (Isa. 9:6). But because of preachers who do not preach the whole Word of God, most people have not heard of the scripture that Jesus speaks when he says,

> "I come not to bring peace into the world, but a sword. For I come to set a man against his father and the daughter against her mother and the daughter-

in-law against her mother-in-law. And a person's enemies shall be of their own household. They who love father or mother more than me are not worthy of me, and they who love son or daughter more than me are not worthy of me. They who take not their own cross and follow me is not worthy of me. They who find their life shall lose it, and they who lose their life, [even like Moses and Paul did], for my name's sake, shall find it." (Matt. 10:33–39; Mic. 7:5–10; Ps. 101:1–4, 7; Prov. 30:11; Rev. 1:10–18; 19:15, 21; Ruth 1; 2 Tim. 2:9 – 13)

True love does not rejoice in or support sin, but true love supports and rejoices in the truth (1 Cor. 13:6). Christ says, "Every house divided against itself shall not stand, and they who are not with me are against me" (Matt. 12:24–30). To clarify, your Christian home will not stand if you allow it to be used for sinful purposes, and in terms of unholy homes and organizations, they will fall whether they stand together or not, because they are not with God. The Bible says that one sinner destroys much good (Eccles. 9:18).

Jesus is called the Lamb of God (John 1:29, 36; Rev. 5:6; 7:17; 14:10; 15:3; 19:9; 21:22, 23; 22:1, 3).

He is also called the Lion of Judah (Gen. 49:9; Rev. 5:5). Thus, Christ in his wrath and conquests is like a Lion, and he is more often like a Lamb when he displays grace and mercy toward us and when he leads, guides, and protects us. When Christ is called the Prince of Peace, he is more like a humble, meek, Lamb (Isa. 9:6). But when Christ says his Word and his tongue is like a sword, then Christ is more like a Lion (Matt. 10:33–39; Mic. 7:5–10; Ps. 101:1–4, 7; Prov. 30:11; Rev. 1:10–18; 19:15, 21).

It seems as if Christ went against his own mother at one point for something that she had done outside of the will of God, and he certainly went against his younger brothers and sisters, the children who Mary birthed after Jesus was born, because they did not believe in him during the same time that the Jews sought to kill him for speaking against the evil practices of the world (Matt. 12:46-50; John 7:1-5). And the Bible clearly says that King Asa removed his mother from being queen because she practiced sin and idolatry (1 Kings 15:12-13). Those scriptures also say, in addition to several other scriptures, that Asa also put all homosexuals and sodomites out of the land because they practiced abomination, including homosexuality and sodomy, like the heathen and pagan nations did, which the Lord cast out (1 Kings 14:22-24; 15:12-13). The homosexuals and sodomites that happened to remain after the days of King Asa, his son, Jehoshaphat, banished from the land when he became king (1 Kings 22:46). King Josiah also rebelled against homosexuals who built their houses next to the house of the Lord (2 Kings 23:7). Again, Levi did not show respect of persons toward his father, mother, brother, or own children, but he demanded that they obey the Word of God (Deut. 33:9).

The Bible says that Christ's friends tried to physically harm him and accuse him of being evil (Mark 3:20-35). Notice those scriptures began with his friends trying to harm him and concluded with what seems like his mother and younger brothers offending him. The Bible tells us to not put our trust in a friend and to not tell certain spouses certain things, because "a person's enemies shall be of their own household" (Matt. 10:33-39; Mic. 7:5-10; Ps. 101:1-4, 7; Prov. 30:11).

Christians should know that the world loves its own people and not the true servants of God, and that the Bible says that a friend of the world is an enemy of God, and that Christians too are enemies of God when they support worldly practices and policies (James 4:2-4; John 1:10-12; 15:18-19; 1 John 2:15-17; 3:13).

Yes, it is possible to be blessed and still be an enemy of God because Christ tells us to love our enemies, just as Christ loves his enemies, and even asked God to forgive the people who killed him (Luke 23:34; Acts 3:12–17). Blessings come to the just and the unjust, the unthankful and the evil, but being blessed with earthly possessions does not mean that a person is saved and on their way to heaven (Deut. 9:4–7; 10:17– 22; Ezek. 29:17–20; Matt. 5:43–48; Luke 6:35; Acts 14:8–18; Ps. 17:13–15; Neh. 9:35–39; Ps. 145:9–10).

People who thank, praise, and glorify God receive blessings from God; and glorifying and praising God is a form of sacrifice unto God but obedience is better than sacrifice (1 Sam. 15:22; Rom. 12:1 – 2; Matt. 9:10 – 13; 23:23; Prov. 21:3; Ps. 4:5; 40:6 – 8: Hos. 6:6; Mic. 6:7; Heb. 13:15).

Jesus was obedient and a sacrifice, including not only when he suffered and died but also when he left his riches in heaven to live in poverty on earth for our sake (2 Cor. 8:9; Phil. 4:19; Lev. 12:6–8; Luke 2:21–24; Rom. 15:1–3).

Not everyone who praises and glorifies God will go to heaven, but they who obey God will inherit the kingdom of God (Matt. 7:21–23; Mic. 3:11).

Psalms 34:1 says, "I will bless the Lord at all times. His praise shall continually be in my mouth." But anyone can praise God and say, "Lord, Lord." That is one reason another scripture says, "Blessed are they who keep justice and who does righteousness at all times" (Ps. 106:3; 119:20). The sword that Christ is talking about is the Word of God (Matt. 10:35). When Christ revealed himself to the Apostle John after the resurrection and ascension, his tongue looked like a sword (Rev. 1:10–18; 19:15, 21). And Christ says to the world, "Repent, before I come and fight against you with the sword of my mouth" (Rev. 2:16). Out of God's mouth comes both trouble and well-being (Lam. 3:38). God also says that he chastises and even punishes the world with the rod of his mouth (2 Thess. 2:8; Isa. 11:1–5). The Bible also says that the Word of God is sharper than any two-edged sword, cutting deep into the bone marrow, soul, and spirit, and is a discerner of the thoughts and intents of the heart (Heb. 4:12). Either we can suffer like Christ for God's sake and righteousness' sake, or we can suffer like a sinner and like a nonbeliever in support of sin, ungodly humans, and the devil (1 Pet. 4:12–19; 2 Tim. 2:8–9; Job 36:21).

We can obey the Lion in Christ, or we will suffer from sins by obeying the devil who God sometimes allows to roam the earth as a roaring lion seeking whom he may deceive and devour (1 Pet. 5:8–9).

We must "be strong in the Lord and the power of his might, put on the whole armor of God in righteousness, on the right hand and on the left hand, that we may be able to withstand in the evil day and having done all to stand. Stand, therefore, having your body covered with truth while wearing the breastplate of righteousness and carrying the sword of the Spirit, which is the Word of God" (Eph. 6:10–17). Be doers of the Word and not just hearers only (James 1:22–27; Matt. 13:1–23; Acts 17:11–12; Ps. 81:10–16; Jer. 15:15–21; Rev. 10:9–11).

OUR HOMES AND FAMILIES MUST BE HOLY AND SANCTIFIED

Some people say Christians are evil for telling them that God says all sinners, especially abominable sinners such as homosexuals, are worthy of death. But the Bible says, "If it seems evil to you to serve the Lord, choose you this day whom you will serve, but as for me and my house, we will serve the Lord" (Josh. 24:15). To God be the glory when there are whole households and whole families serving Christ in holiness (Gen. 18:17–19; Acts 18:7–8; 1 Tim. 3:1–13).

God said regarding Abraham after he promised Abraham that the nation of Israel will come from his seed, "Shall I hide from Abraham what I am about to do? I know him, he will command his children and his household after him, and they shall keep the way of the Lord to do justice" (Gen. 18:17–19). And as was with Jacob's son Joseph when he was a slave in Egypt, the Lord blessed the king's household for Joseph's sake because Joseph was righteous and because Joseph did not sleep with the slave master's wife after she tried hard to seduce him (Gen. 39). Notice that the king who was also the slave master favored Joseph, so the king's household was blessed for Joseph's sake and because the heathen king favored Joseph. And even after the king's wife lied and said that Joseph tried to rape her, Joseph was cast into prison, but the inmates and the prison guards favored Joseph too, because God was with him (Gen. 39). And Joseph continued to be favored after he was released from prison (Gen. 40, 41).

JOEL OSTEEN AND OTHER HYPOCRITE PREACHERS CAUSED DEATH

President Obama had the audacity and the nerves to put his hands on two Bibles during his second inauguration, including the former Bible of President Lincoln and the former Bible of Dr. Martin Luther King, Jr.

Joel Osteen, a televangelist, and pastor of the largest church in America during the early twenty-first century, had the evil nerves to inaugurate a lesbian mayor in the city of Houston, Texas, while placing the hand of the incoming gay mayor on the Bible, and he put the mayor's gay girlfriend's hand on top of the incoming mayor's hand. That was a huge and public hypocrite preacher performance. Joel Osteen also had the nerve to charge thousands of people each week admissions to enter his church, like at sporting events. Joel Osteen entertained people while he lied and told them what they wanted to hear and not the whole Word of God, which includes more warnings than blessings. Joel Osteen also made plenty of money from selling feel good books that do not mirror the Bible that has far more warnings in it from God than it has blessings from God. Warnings from God are blessings too when we take heed to God's warnings.

It is things like what Joel Osteen did that caused many people to not trust preachers and churches. Sinners and nonbelievers are sinners, but they know a hypocrite when they see one. The television talk show host Larry King of *Larry King Live* interviewed Joel Osteen. Larry King did not believe in God, but he mildly asked Joel Osteen if what he did with the gay mayor was aligned with the Bible. Joel Osteen made excuses, but Larry King knew better even though he did not believe in God. As stated earlier, Joel Osteen had the largest church in the United States, but the Bible says that many people run with itching ears to lying preachers and to preachers who do not correct or rebuke them, like Joel Osteen (2 Tim. 4:2–3; Prov. 17:3– 4). Many shall follow them, and the way of truth shall be evil spoken of (2 Pet. 2:1–2). This is evident when supporters of homosexuality speak evil of people who use Bible scriptures to speak against and to stand against homosexuality. King Asa put a prophet in prison for telling him the truth about God (2 Chron. 16:9–10).

In August of 2017, the lesbian was no longer the mayor of Houston, Texas, but God's wrath finally hit the city of Houston with a mighty and terrible hurricane and flood that punished the people for electing a gay mayor and for following one of the biggest hypocrite preachers in the United States, Joel Osteen. The Bible tells us that God in his wrath is terrible (Exod. 34:10; Deut. 7:21; 10:17; Neh. 1:5; 4:14; 9:32; Job 37:22; Ps. 47:2; Jer. 20:11).

God says he will not again destroy the world with water like he did in Noah's lifetime, because human hearts are evil from youth and that they will only sin more and more (Gen. 8:19–22; Isa. 1:4– 5; 47:12, 15; 48:8; Jer. 22:21).

God says that some people corrupt themselves to the point that their whole head is sick, a sinful nation, laden with iniquity and sins, who have forsaken the Lord and provoked the Holy One to anger (Isa. 1:4–5). So God causes what people call natural disasters in different places until the world is finally destroyed by fire (Gen. 9:8–17; 2 Pet. 3:4–14).

Although there were other places that God destroyed as he did Sodom and Gomorrah, God did not totally destroy New York in 2001 and New Orleans in 2005 as he did Sodom and Gomorrah. He did not totally destroy the areas of Asia during the great tsunami of 2004. And he did not totally destroy Houston, Texas, with a great flood as punishment for their sins, for electing a gay mayor a few years earlier, and for following one of the biggest hypocrite preachers in America, Joel Osteen.

God is a Spirit, and they who worship him must worship him in spirit and in truth, for the Father seeks such to worship him (John 4:23–24; Zech. 8:1–8). Some people have known, and others still know the depths of Satan (Rev. 2:24). We must search the deep things of God, comparing spiritual with spiritual, because natural-thinking people cannot understand the things of the Spirit of God, because it is foolishness to them, but sanctified Christians have the mind of Christ (1 Cor. 1:10; 2:9–16; Rom. 15:5–6). True religion is to go unspotted from the world (James 1:26–27). Joel Osteen and Barack Obama were enemies of God and were friends of the world. Lovers of the world love their own people, and a friend of the world including those who agree with the world and accept worldly beliefs are enemies of God (James 4:4; John 15:17–19).

SOME CHRISTIANS POLLUTE GOD'S HOUSE OF WORSHIP

President Obama and his administration in January of 2013 determined that the Washington National Cathedral where politicians go to mourn tragedies and to celebrate presidents will perform same-sex marriages. That is even worse than Pastor Joel Osteen inaugurating a lesbian mayor in Houston, Texas, while placing her hands and her girlfriend's hands on the Bible. They have no fear, reverence, or respect for God, the house of the Lord, or the Bible. By doing this, the Obama administration and the hypocrite preachers were totally disregarding God. That is one reason tragedies keep happening and it is one reason Muslims and people in other religions do not think much of Christians. Most Muslims are not terrorists or extremists, but God uses Muslim extremists to punish Christians just as he used the Babylonians and Persians to punish the Hebrews and Jews in the Bible.

The Bible says concerning people who defile the house of God,

> "Both prophet and preacher are profane. Yes, in my house I have found their wickedness," says the Lord. "Their way shall be unto them as slippery ways in the darkness, for I shall bring evil upon them, even the year of their visitation," says the Lord. "They strengthened the hands of evildoers, that none return from their

wickedness. They all are unto me as Sodom, and the inhabitants thereof as Gomorrah. Listen not to the words of the prophets [and preachers]. They speak a vision of their own heart and not out of the mouth of the Lord. They continue to say to them who despise me, 'The Lord has said you shall have peace.' And they say unto everyone who walks after the imagination of their own heart, no evil shall come upon you. For who has stood in the counsel of the Lord and heard his Word? Who has marked his Word, and heard it? The anger of the Lord shall not return, until he has executed, and until he has performed the thoughts of his heart. In the latter days you shall consider it perfectly. But if they had stood in my counsel, and had caused my people to hear my words, then they should have turned them from their evil way and from the evil of their doings. They are prophets [and preachers] of the deceit of their own heart. Is not my Word like as a fire," says the Lord, "and like a hammer that breaks the rock in pieces?" (Jer. 23:11–29)

At one point in the Bible, the house of God became so profane that God burned it to the ground and he allowed all the precious gold, silver, and precious art to be taken away by a heathen nation (2 Chron. 36:14–20; 29:5; Lam. 2:7; Jer. 52:13; Isa. 64:4–12; 2 Kings 24:1–2, 11–13; 12:18; 14:14; 25:13; 1 Kings 14:26; 15:18).

At another time, a certain king thought so little of the house of God that he gave its gold away to save his own life (2 Kings 16:5–9). Even as far back as the tabernacle, people defiled it and God killed them for doing so (1 Sam. 2:22–25). So, whether it is a tabernacle, a temple, a house of God, or a church house, if you do in it things opposite of God's Word, you are jeopardizing your life and putting yourself in danger of eternal life in hell.

Before God allowed Solomon to build the house of God, David said, "The temple is not for mankind, but for the Lord" (1 Chron.

29:1). God says,

> You trust in lying words, that cannot profit. Will you commit sin and come and stand before me in this house, which is called by my name, and say, 'We shall be delivered while we commit abominations, including homosexuality, that God hates?' Has this house which is called by my name become a den of robbers in your eyes? Behold, even I have seen it," says the Lord. "But go unto my place which was in Shiloh, where I set my name at first, and see what I did to it for the wickedness of my people Israel. And now, because ye have done all these works," says the Lord, "and I spoke unto you, rising early and speaking, but you heard me not, and I called you, but you answered not. Therefore, I will do unto this house, which is called by my name, the place you trust in, as I have done unto Shiloh. And I will cast you out of my sight. (Jer. 7:8–16)

OUR BODIES ARE TEMPLES OF GOD, BUT GOD DOES NOT DWELL INSIDE DEFILED TEMPLES

Nowadays, the temple of God is the human body. Jesus and Peter described their body as temples (John 2:19–21; 2 Cor. 5:1; 2 Pet. 1:12–15; Heb. 9:11).

God does not dwell in temples made with hands, but in holy and sanctified humans (Acts 7:48; 17:24). If anyone defiles the temple of God with sin, God shall destroy that person someday, sooner or later, whether they defile the body with drugs, cigarettes, too much alcohol, too much food, the wrong kinds of food, heterosexual fornication and adultery, homosexuality, sex changes, or cross dressing like the opposite sex (1 Cor. 3:16–23; 6:9– 20; Eph. 2:19–22; Heb. 3:4–19; 4:1; Rom. 6:23).

Notice that sins other than homosexual sins can also cause a person to die and go to hell. The biggest difference nowadays is that most people will admit that fornication and adultery are sins and are wrong and that admission alone acknowledges God, but politicians, some preachers, some so-called Christians, and certain other people in society say homosexuality is not wrong. That is what gets the nation and the world in trouble with

God. "Know ye not that unrighteous people shall not inherit the kingdom of God? Be not deceived, neither fornicators, nor idolaters, nor adulterers, nor homosexuals shall inherit the kingdom of God" (1 Cor. 6:9–11). Also, murderers, nonbelievers, workers of abomination, sorcerers, whoremongers, idolaters, and all liars shall have their part in the lake of fire (Rev. 21:7–8, 27; 22:14–15).

GOD DOES NOT DWELL INSIDE UNCLEAN TEMPLES, BUT DEMONS DO

The Lord will not dwell in an unclean temple, but Satan will. Satan will also dwell in an empty temple or empty body too. And if you have ever had a demon or unclean spirit of drugs, alcohol, sex, homosexuality, or any other sin, when the Lord cast it out of your body and you do not allow Christ to fill your body with the Holy Ghost, also called the Holy Spirit, the unclean spirit, also called a demon, will return with seven more evil spirits, for a total of eight (Matt. 12:43–45). If you had two evil spirits dwelling in you and God cast them out, each one will return with seven more, for a total of sixteen demons dwelling inside of you. If you had three demons and you do not allow God to fill you with the Holy Spirit, the three demons will return with twenty-one more demons, for a total of twenty-four, and the number gets higher based on how many demons were cast out in the first place. And your new condition will be worse than your former condition (John 5:14; 2 Pet. 2:20; Isa. 57:11–12; Matt. 12:43–45).

One man in the Bible had so many unclean and evil spirits inside of him that the demon called himself Legion, because the demons inside of the man were many (Mark 5:1–20). The same applies to the demon of cocaine and other drugs, prostitution, fornication, adultery, murder, child molestation, and homosexuality. Also, remember, if a former drug addict, for example, or anyone decides to help a person who is currently using or selling drugs, they must be careful not to be tempted themselves (Gal. 6:1).

The Bible clearly states, "Know you not that you are the temple of God, and that the Spirit of God dwells in you? If anyone defiles the temple of God, God shall destroy that person, for the temple of God is holy which temple you are" (1 Cor. 3:16–23; 6:9–20; Eph. 2:19–22; Heb. 3:4–19; 4:1; Rom. 6:23).

Just as God destroyed the precious temple with fire in the Old Testament that Solomon built because people sinned in it, he destroys human temples in this day and age, and he preserves hell's fire for them when they rise from the dead (2 Chron. 29:5; 36:14–20; Lam. 2:7; Jer. 52:13; Isa. 64:4–12).

The Bible states, "Meats for the belly, and the belly for meats, but God shall destroy both it and the people who eat the meats" (1 Cor. 6:13–17).

GAY COUPLES ARE NOT BRIDES OF CHRIST AND ARE NOT ONE WITH CHRIST

The body is not for fornication or homosexuality, but for the Lord, and the Lord for the body. "Know ye not that your bodies are the members of Christ? Shall I then take the members of Christ, and make them members of a whore? God forbids. What? Know ye not that they who are joined to a whore are one body? For two, says God, shall be one flesh. But they who are joined unto the Lord are one spirit" (1 Cor. 6:13–17).

When God said two shall be one flesh, he was directly and specifically speaking to Adam and Eve, man and woman, and telling future generations to leave their father and mother and take a wife and a husband (Gen. 2:24; Matt. 19:5; 1 Cor. 6:16).

God did not say that we must leave our two fathers or two mothers and marry people of the same sex (Gen. 2:23–24). Therefore, if a man should marry another man or a woman should marry another woman, it is worse than a man marrying a whorish woman, or a woman marrying a whorish man. He also says not to marry people of the same sex, for not only is it more sinful to marry a person of the same sex, but also it is abomination. When people of the same sex marry each other, they are not one with Christ because they defile and disobey

God's Word, but they are also not one with their gay mate either because there is no such thing as a gay marriage in the sight of God.

The church itself in this generation is the body of Christ, so when you join a church nowadays, you are committing to becoming part of Christ's body and to becoming Christ's bride, unless you join a hypocrite church (Rev. 19:7; 21:2, 9; 22:17; 2 Cor. 11:2–3; Eph. 5:23, 27; Isa. 54:4–10; Jer. 31:27–37).

People cannot be a bride of Christ when they call him a lie by saying gays can marry and by committing other forms of sin and living in those sins. Again, true religion according to the Bible is to go unspotted from the world (James 1:26–27). And Christ shall return for a church without spot, wrinkle, or blemish (Eph. 5:1–28; 1 Pet. 1:13–19; 2 Pet. 3:1–14; 1 Tim. 6:3–16; Jude 1:22–24).

The true church and true foundation of God is the body of Christ; and true, holy, and sanctified people are members of his body and members of his church; and everyone else who confesses the name of Christ must also depart from sin, because the foundation stands sure and does not waver (2 Tim. 2:19). The Bible says that there is only one foundation of Christ, and we must take heed how we add to the foundation (1 Cor. 3:10–15). Gay people and their supporters reject Christ, his body, and his foundation; but Christ the Stone, which the builders rejected, has become the chief cornerstone that holds up God-fearing people (Isa. 28:16; Ps. 118:17–24; Matt. 21:42; Acts 4:10–11; 1 Pet. 2:6–7).

Christ told Peter that he was the rock upon which the church would be built and that the gates of hell shall not prevail against it, nor will homosexuality prevail against it (Matt. 16:18–19; John 3:3–7; Acts 2:36–39; 8:14–17; 10:42–48; 19:1–6).

Some Protestant and non – Catholic people also name their churches after the apostles or the works of the apostles such as St. Paul, St. Peter Missionary Baptist Church, and St. James, or Antioch Baptist Church, Antioch being where the apostle's doctrine was strongly preached and where the followers of Christ were supposedly first called Christians (Acts 11:26 – 27). And some Protestant and non – Catholic churches are named Rock of Ages, but Christ said that Peter is the rock upon which the church would be established, and the gates of hell shall not prevail against it (Matt. 16:18 – 19). Peter then established the first church in history by baptizing people in the name of the Lord Jesus Christ. Therefore, any church that is named after Christ's original apostles or has the word rock in its name should certainly baptize people like the original apostles baptized, and that is in the name of the Lord Jesus Christ (John 3:3 – 7; Acts 2:36 – 41; 8:14 – 17; 10:47 – 48; 19:2 – 5).

Even the people who are prayed to by Catholics must do what the original apostles did in regard to baptism and living a holy and sanctified life unto the Lord, because the saints and apostles who the churches are named for were apostolic and the apostles were baptized in the name of the Lord Jesus Christ (Acts 2:36 – 41; 8:14 – 17; 10:47 – 48; 19:2 – 5; John 3:1 – 7).

Some churches are even named after men from this generation. That is totally unacceptable, because Christ said in his humility, "No one is good but Father God" (Matt. 19:17). And to name a church after a human is to also take glory away from the Lord Father God Almighty.

The church body of Christ is different from a church house that houses his people during church services. When people allow homosexuality in the church house, the church temple of their body defiles the church house and their own body. Again, the human body is the temple of God and the Spirit of God dwells in it; we do not belong to ourselves, but to God (1 Cor. 3:16–23; 6:9–20; Eph. 2:19–22; Heb. 3:4–19; 4:1; Rom. 6:23). Some humans still say in error about certain other humans, "To each their own."

If anyone does not have the Spirit of Christ, that person does not belong to Christ (Rom. 8:9). They belong to their father, the devil, who is the father of lies (John 8:42–47; Mic. 4:5; 1 Tim. 5:15).

Some people even confess Christ, but Jesus will say on judgment day that he does not know them as holy servants and shut the door, just like in the days of Noah when God shut the door to the ark and the flood killed everyone in the world except Noah's family of eight people (Luke 13:24–27; Matt. 7:21–23). If every dead person is already in heaven or hell, why is Christ coming to earth a second time? The answer is that when we die, we do not go straight to heaven or hell, but we remain dead until Christ's second coming (Dan. 12:1 – 3; 1 Thess. 4:13 – 18; 2 Thess. 1:7–9; 1 Cor. 15:50 – 53; Rev. 20:13; Eccles. 12:7; Gen. 2:7).

The Bible also says that even though the Lord is high, he considers the lowly, but the proud he knows afar off (Ps. 138:6). But after you receive the Holy Ghost, the Bible says, "Greater is Christ in you, than they who are in the world" (1 John 4:4). And supporters of homosexuality including President Obama and homosexuals themselves are of the world.

NOT ALL SINS ARE THE SAME AND GOD PUNISHES SOME SINS HARDER THAN OTHER SINS

Some people say all sins are the same but that is not correct. For example, Jesus says if anyone hurts a child who believes in him, that person would do better to tie a weight around their neck and jump into the sea, rather than suffer what God has for them, and that children have special angels just for them who visits God face to face often (Matt. 18:3–6, 10). Christ embraced a child in his arms and said unto his disciples, "Whosoever shall receive a child in the name of Jesus receives Jesus" (Mark 9:36–37).

As indicated earlier, abomination is also a different kind of sin too.

There are seven things that God hates and that are abomination. And most of the seven—if not all—can relate to homosexuality, especially if you say it is all right for people to be gay and to marry other gay people (Prov. 6:16–19).

1. A proud look. Gays are now proud and not ashamed of their homosexuality.
2. A lying tongue. Gays, some preachers, and some Christians

are lying on God by saying they were born that way and that it is all right to be gay, to marry other gay people, and to adopt children. They were not born that way. God made them, and they made a choice to be gay, or someone else perverted them.
3. Hands that shed innocent blood. Politicians like President Obama and some preachers have blood on their hands because they lie on God by telling the people it is all right to be gay, while they live and die in their sins (Jer. 5:12; 2 Chron. 19).

4. A heart that has wicked imaginations. God cast down imaginations that are against him, and gay people and their supporters imagine evil against God and against his true servants. The Word of God says that his true servants are set over the whole world by God to root up, to pull down, to destroy, to throw down, and to plant (Jer. 1:10). The weapons of our warfare are not carnal or earthly, but mighty through God to the pulling down of strongholds, casting down imaginations, and every high thing that exalts itself against the knowledge of God and bringing into captivity every thought to the obedience of Christ (2 Cor. 10:4–6).
5. Feet that are quick to run to mischief. Members of the media run to a gay story because they make money off the story and some of them are gay too.
6. A false witness that speaks lies. This is relatively the same as number two.
7. They who sow discord among brethren. The fact that President Obama and his administration preferred that everyone accept homosexuality and allowed them to marry in certain churches, including the Washington National Cathedral, caused some Christians to be divided because some of them listened to Obama and not to God.

Therefore, when people say all sins are the same, they are incorrect. All sins are the same in terms of God forgiving us, but they are not the same in terms of how God punishes us.

To clarify, if a sinner, an evil person, or a wicked person truly repents and turns from their sins, God will forgive them. Christ will forgive a murderer, a whore, a drug dealer, a rapist, a child molester, or gay person just as fast as he would forgive a child for taking a cookie out of a cookie jar. But the murderer and child molester, for example, will be punished greater than the kid who took a cookie from a cookie jar. And there still may be a certain type of punishment after repenting. That all depends on God, just as when David repented in the book of Psalms more than most people ever repented (Ps. 38:1–4). God forgave David, but he was still punished (2 Sam. 12:7–14; 24:1–24; 1 Chron. 21:1, 9–14).

Another sin that is different from other sins is to not forgive, which is also punished differently. If we do not forgive others, God will not forgive us (Matt. 6:13–15; 18:23–35; Mark 11:25–26; Amos 1:11; Col. 3:12–13; Eph. 4:31–32; Luke 6:36–37).

Therefore, we must forgive homosexuals but still stand against the sin of homosexuality. "Adultery is a worse sin than fornication, because fornication causes us to sin against God and our own bodies" (1 Cor. 6:13–20). But adultery is sin against God, the participants of adultery, and the families who suffer from extramarital relationships, and adultery is dishonorable and destroys the soul. Also, if a child is conceived in adultery, that hurts both families and the child could end up being raised without one biological parent and viewed as a bastard or illegitimate child by other people" (Prov. 6:32–35). All sin is not the same. We all are sinners, but we all are not evil or wicked, so evil and wickedness are different and greater sins. Jesus also says, "All manner of sin and blasphemy shall be forgiven, but blasphemy against the Holy Ghost shall not be forgiven" (Matt. 12:31). So once again, all sin is not the same, but the blood of Jesus Christ, the Son of God, cleans us from all other sin (1 John 1:7–10). People who are guilty of blasphemy against the Holy Ghost may still go to heaven, but they will not be forgiven, which means they would have a lesser rank in heaven (Matt. 5:18–19;

11:11; 20:20–23; Jude 1:9; 1 Thess. 4:16; Dan. 12:1–3; 1 Tim. 5:21; Heb. 1:4; Eph. 1:21).

As stated earlier, the Bible says that homosexuality is an abomination, and all workers of abomination are cursed and will go to hell to burn in eternal fire, unless they repent and turn from the sin of homosexuality (Rev. 21:8, 27; 22:14–15). People who accept and allow homosexuality in their churches, homes, hotels, and other facilities are in jeopardy of God's wrath. God says, "Thou shall not bring an abomination into your house, or you will become cursed like it" (Deut. 7:26).

WE MUST NOT SUPPORT UNGODLY POLITICS SIMPLY FOR WORLDLY GAIN

People who accept and support unrighteous politicians instead of God's Word, because the politician will make life better in one sense, are in jeopardy of losing their soul to hell's fire forever. Moses was raised by the daughter of a king of Egypt, but he refused to be called a prince of Egypt and chose to suffer in a hot barren desert with God's people, and like Christ, instead of enjoying the pleasures of sin for a season (Heb. 11:24–27). We must deny ourselves as well of sin and of the support of homosexuality and any other sin, just as Moses denied himself of riches and royalty (Luke 9:23–26). That would be like the daughters of Barack Obama refusing to live in the White House because their dad supported homosexuality but instead chose to live in a hot desert for years until God gave them instructions to go back to Washington D.C. to rebuke their father Barak Obama and the entire nation.

They would have walked away from maids, servants, butlers, and all the luxuries of being a child of the president, to live in a hot desert for God's sake. Moses left a rich life and a life of being a politician in Egypt, which was the greatest nation in the world at that time, to lead slaves out of bondage who were God's people (Acts 7:20-37; Heb. 11:24-27). That is what Moses did. And you also must deny yourself for the Lord's sake (Luke 9:23-26). Christ was oppressed and lived in poverty his whole life, but he never supported anti-God politics, because spirituality supersedes equality.

The Apostle Paul left a prosperous life as a politician and became a poor man for God's sake. Therefore, Paul was raised as a Hebrew but born in Rome, which was the greatest nation in the world at that time, but he walked away from all of his riches and political power in Rome to become a Christian (Acts 22:1-10, 19-20, 25-30; 23:6; 26:5-18; Phil. 3:5-11; 2 Cor. 11:22; Acts 9:10-16).

Not only did Paul leave a prosperous life of politics, but also, he suffered greatly for standing up for the Word of God. The Apostle Paul said, "In labors more abundant, in beatings above measure, in prisons more often than others who say they stand for God's Word. Of the Jews I was beaten and receive 39 licks with a whip five different times, three times I was beaten with a rod, I was stoned once, shipwrecked three times, and floated in the ocean a day and a night. I have been in danger of robbers, my own countrymen, heathens, and false brothers. I have hungered and thirsted, I have fasted often, and I have suffered in cold weather without proper clothing to keep me warm." (2 Cor. 11:23-33). Now ask yourself, what have you done to stand against homosexuality and other sins?

Phil Roberts of a television reality show in December 2013 denied himself by refusing to retract his biblical statements against homosexuality. The television show's producers suspended him from the show. Most people on television change their story after being pressured and after they realize how much money they may lose, but Phil Roberts basically told the producers of the show that they can cancel the show and keep their money, because he would continue to stand with God. The producers allowed him to return to the show because they realized that without that Christian man, they would lose more money than he would. All television personalities must do the same thing instead of planting their seed in weak soil and backing away from their statements because the anti-God supporters of homosexuality pressure them (Matt. 13:1–23, 43; Luke 8:4–8; Acts 17:11–12; James 1:22–27).

Ask yourself, what have you sacrificed and stood against to love, fear, serve, and support the Lord?

"What profits a person if they gain the whole world, and lose their soul, or what would you give in exchange for your soul? Whosoever in this adulterous and sinful generation shall be ashamed of Christ and the Word of God, Christ will be ashamed of them" (Mark 8:34–38; Matt. 24:3–14; Job 27:8; 1 Thess. 2:2; 2 Tim. 1:12; James 1:8–27; Rev. 3:1–6).

The Apostle Paul wrote, "I urge, first of all, that petitions, prayers, intercessions and thanksgiving be made for all people, for kings and all people in authority, that we may live peaceful and quiet lives in all godliness and holiness" (1 Tim. 2:1–2). "Pursue peace with all people, and holiness, for without holiness no one can see the Lord, being diligent in the Word of God, or you may fall short of the grace of God" (Heb. 12:12–15). "Let us cleanse ourselves from all filthiness of the flesh and spirit, perfecting holiness in the fear of God" (2 Cor. 7:1). The Bible tells us to not put a wicked thing before our eyes and to not support people who turn aside from the Word of God (Ps. 101:3–4).

SPIRITUALITY SUPERSEDES EQUALITY

When Pres. Barack Obama announced that gay people should have the right to marry, some people continued to support him because they did not want a member of another party—or in the case of most black people, they did not want a white person—to take the office. But spirituality supersedes equality. Spirit also supersedes civil rights, color, race, and political and religious affiliation. When any person goes against God's Word to support a person because of his or her race, they have "changed the truth of God into a lie and worshipped and served the creature more than the Creator" (Rom. 1:24–25).

When we support politicians and presidents and their homosexual policies and beliefs, that is modern-day idolatry; and idolatry is to give more respect, love, honor, glory, time, praise, worship, fear, obedience, or admiration to anything or anyone than you give to Christ. Idolatry is also to neglect to do things for Christ because you are committed to or addicted to other things or to place yourself or your race above others (Acts 4:19; Jer. 2:13–14). And the Bible says, "No idolater will inherit the kingdom of heaven" (Eph. 5:5; 1 Cor. 6:9; Rev. 21:8, 27; 22:14–15; Gal. 5:19–21; Ezek. 23:29).

To covet something that belongs to another person is also idolatry (Eph. 5:5). God says people who have idols shall bear the sins of their idol, which also means they suffer for those sins and die in those sins, just like their idol, unless they repent (Ezek. 23:49). When people turn their back on God, they commit at least two sins, turning their back on God and serving another person, gods, or things, adding sin to sin (Jer. 2:13–14; Judg. 10:10; Isa. 30:1; 1 Sam. 12:19). Idolatry can also be the possessing or displaying of an image that other people idolize while knowing that person or thing has become an idol to many people. At that point, Christians should remove the image or the picture.

Rebellion is as the sin of witchcraft and stubbornness and covetousness are the same as the sin of idolatry (1 Sam. 15:23; Col. 3:1–6), because you would be rejecting the Word of the Lord like a participant of voodoo, sorcery, and witchcraft rejects God to be part of those evil practices. And when people are stubborn, they are holding on to sin instead of committing to Christ, so God may reject them too (1 Sam. 15:23).

GAY ANIMALS

God made animals before he made humans. But animals do not desire to have sex with any animal of the same sex (Isa. 1:3–10; Job 34:27; Hosea 7:2).

When God destroyed the earth with water, he told Noah to take male and female animals with him (Gen. 7:16). He also took his three sons and their three wives to repopulate the earth. He did not take two males of the same sex. Nor did he take two females of the same sex, because they cannot reproduce and their sex organs were not made to fit comfortably, or conveniently.

SOME BLACK PEOPLE REJECTED GOD BECAUSE OBAMA WAS BLACK

Christians who supported Pres. Barack Obama are like the people of Israel when they made the golden calf in the wilderness. And to suffer financially, economically, or in any other way is nothing compared to facing God's wrath of disasters and tragedies sent from heaven, not to mention hell as the ultimate punishment. And none of us have forfeited a royal, rich, position as Moses did. In other words, Moses chose to suffer than to support an unrighteous political system and king. Besides, when people who supported Barack Obama became sick or when they were on their deathbed, President Obama did not visit most people, but Christ will visit anyone who calls upon his name (Jer. 29:12–13; Rom. 10:9–11). So it would behoove people to choose Christ over a human. Again, the Bible says, "Choose ye this day whom ye will serve, but as for me and my house, we will serve the Lord" (Josh. 24:15).

On the 60th anniversary of the March on Washington that was led by the great Dr. Martin Luther King, Jr., at least two of his children in August 2023 gathered in Washington D.C. to commemorate the march, but they spoke in support of gay marriage. Their behavior on that day caused them to be abominable, antichrist, hypocrite Christians, according to what the Bible says. There is no record of Dr. King supporting gay marriage, but his widow Coretta Scott King did support gay marriage before she died. It is a shame and a disgrace that such a great family ended up supporting anti-God practices and policies after the entire American Civil Rights Movement was done in the name, humility, meekness, peace, and holiness of Christ.

Although black people were treated wrongly and their babies were taken from them and sold to other slave masters, at least their babies were alive. When news spread that the baby Jesus had been born, in efforts to destroy him while he was a baby, every firstborn male in the entire land two years old and under was killed (Matt. 2:1–20). And when Moses was born in Egypt, every firstborn baby in the land was killed in efforts to prevent the Hebrew slave population from outgrowing the Egyptian population (Exod. 1:8–22; 2:1–10).

BLACK PEOPLES' FIGHT FOR CIVIL RIGHTS DO NOT COMPARE TO THE FIGHT FOR GAY RIGHTS

When black people join the Christian family, they must understand that Martin Luther King, Medgar Evers, and Emmett Till were killed for equality on earth, and equality was indeed ordained by God. Meanwhile Christ, John the Baptist, Paul, James, Stephen, and the firstborn babies when Jesus and Moses were infants, among others, were killed for spirituality and not for earthly equality, but for God's sake, for the kingdom of heaven, for the saving of your soul, and not for just an earthly gift. So gay people should not compare themselves to black people's suffering.

As of February 26, 2020, in the United States, lynching was still not a hate crime, but to kill a homosexual is considered a hate crime. They both should have been hate crimes. But that disparity illustrates that racism is still alive in the United States and that the demonic sin of homosexuality is supported by even some Christians. Most gay people have never been enslaved in chains, taken from their homeland, sold to cruel masters, or had their children and spouses sold into slavery in another part of the world. The Bible says that Christians should seek a better country, in heaven, and not seek our own will (Heb. 11:13–16; 1 Tim. 6:9–10; James 3:13–16; John 5:41, 44; 1 Cor. 13:5).

The people in those scriptures all died in the faith, not having received the promises of Christ, because Christ had not been sacrificed yet; but having seen them afar off, they were persuaded by the Word of God that the holy prophets of the Old Testament wrote, and they embraced the prophecies and confessed that they were only visitors and pilgrims on earth. They desired a better country, in heaven, for God has prepared for them a city (Heb. 11:13–16; Phil. 3:20).

To God, all nations are nothing, even less than nothing (Isa. 40:17).

Lastly, women have made great and deserved advancements, achievements, and accomplishments in the world, and we see women in major positions. But most people do not say that the Women's Liberation Movement should be compared to the Gay Rights Movement, like some people compare the Gay Rights Movement to the American Civil Rights Movement that was led by African Americans. Some people attempt to correlate anything evil or less desirable to black people, for political reasons.

MOST BLACK PEOPLE DO NOT WANT TO BE COMPARED TO GAYS

It is an insult to most black people to be compared to gay people regarding their struggles and their rights. God says, "Thou shall not be gay," but God did not say, "Thou shall not be black." And most black people cannot hide the fact that they are black, but most gay people can conceal the fact that they are gay, whether people assume that they are gay or not. Black people were born black, and no matter what happens, they remain black for the rest of their life, but some gay people change and decide not be gay anymore. When a black person is called the N-word, some people say that it is the same as calling a homosexual gay. That's not true because although some blacks call themselves the N-word, it is not what they are unless they insist that they are, but self-proclaimed homosexuals who are called gay are indeed gay and many gay people are now proud to be called gay. But most black people are not proud to be called the N-word. Women fought for their rights too, but women were born female.

Throughout history, certain people have been sent into slavery against God's will, but some were also sent into slavery because it was God's will (Gen. 15:13–14; Deut. 26:5–11; Acts 7:6; Neh. 9:36–37; Jer. 40:1–3).

However, God has never sent anyone into homosexuality. That is a choice people make or they are enticed or trained to be gay by mankind and by Satan.

Feminine boys and masculine girls must be taught to act more like a boy and more like a girl, respectively, and that is what happened traditionally in the past. Nowadays, some people say it is wrong to teach a boy to be masculine and a girl to be feminine. And predators are taking advantage of them by molesting and raping them. That is one reason we have so many masculine males who secretly participate in homosexuality, and that is one reason we have so many gay people, females included, whether in secret or openly. They are being taught by society that it is okay for boys to be feminine, for girls to be masculine, and for either to be gay. And yes, there is a scripture in the Authorized King James Version of the Bible that says that it is a sin for a man to act feminine or soft, even if he is not gay (1 Cor. 6:9). So, it is a sin to be what some people would call a sissy.

HOMOSEXUALITY IS FLESHLY AND DEMONIC AND IS AGAINST THE SPIRIT OF GOD

Christians who voted for President Obama must understand that Mr. Obama was not God, but flesh and blood, and when he endorsed homosexual marriage, he did not speak through the Spirit, but through the flesh and maybe even through a demonic spirit. The Bible says, "The Spirit is against the flesh, and the flesh is against the Spirit" (Gal. 5:16–24; 1 Pet. 2:11–12). We must abstain from fleshly lust that war against the soul (1 Pet. 2:11). The spirit of humans is willing, but the flesh is weak (Matt. 26:41). But when people allow Christ to do so, he strengthens and settles them (1 Pet. 5:6–11; Ps. 3:5; 55:22). When the word Spirit is capitalized, it always refers to God Almighty and to Christ, and when the word spirit is not capitalized, it always refers to a human spirit, an angel, a demonic spirit, an idol god, and all other spirits.

Flesh and blood cannot inherit the kingdom of heaven but walking and living in the Spirit while you are alive and being changed to a heavenly spirit on judgment day are the ways to inherit heaven (1 Cor. 15:42–52; Gal. 5:16; 24–25; 1 Thess. 4:14–

17).

We reap what we sow (Rom. 2:4–11; Gal. 6:7–10). We must be born of the water and of the Spirit, or we cannot go to heaven (John 3:3–7). Therefore, we must worship God in spirit and in truth and not in the flesh or as a lover of the world (John 4:23–24; Zech. 8:1–8).

And just as the Spirit is against the flesh and the flesh is against the Spirit, the world does not love God's people, and they are enemies of God and of sanctified Christians (James 4:2–4; John 1:10–12; 15:18–19; 1 John 2:15–17; 3:13).

People who are in the flesh cannot please God (Rom. 8:8). When we sow to the flesh, we reap trouble to the flesh, but people who sow to the Spirit shall reap everlasting life in heaven (Gal. 6:7–8). The fruit of the Spirit is goodness, righteousness, and truth, and it is a shame to even speak of in a glorifying manner the fleshly sins that sinners do (Eph. 5:9–12).

.

GAY RIGHTS CAME EASIER THAN CIVIL RIGHTS BECAUSE EVIL LOVES ITS OWN PEOPLE

Black people must remember that gay rights activists pushed harder worldwide than the nations of the world pushed to free African Americans from slavery and to help African-Americans obtain civil rights, human rights, and equality. Black people obtained their rights through Christ and Christian leaders such as Dr. Martin Luther King Jr. and others, and with help from more white people than we know. So gay activists pushed harder to support a sinful, sick, and demonic spirit of homosexuality, while black people suffered and still suffer. One reason the world did not support black people in their conquest to be equal is because homosexuality is a powerful fleshly spirit and sometimes even a demonic spirit, and the other reason is the love of money. Also, either the larger population of activists were gay themselves or they were afraid that they would lose money and business deals if they did not support gay rights. Evil people gain money by oppressing black people, and lovers of the world and the corporate world realized that they would gain even more money by not oppressing gay people (James 4:2–4;

John 1:10–12; 15:18–19; 1 John 2:15–17; 3:13).

SOME PEOPLE SUPPORT GAYS ONLY FOR MONEY & POWER

One reason homosexuality is accepted by some people is because people in high places with plenty of money who own Internet sites and radio and TV shows endorse it and use their power to deceive people. Even TV producers who do not believe in homosexuality sometimes highlight it and create gay shows for filthy money's sake (Titus 1:10–11). Again, the love of money is the root of all evil (1 Cor. 6:9–11; 1 Tim. 6:9–10; 2 Kings 5:15–27). President Barack Obama supported homosexuality and abortions because he knew that doing so would cause him to be reelected.

BAD & EVIL DECISIONS BY LEADERS CAUSE NATIONS TO SUFFER

President Obama caused the whole country to suffer for the sins that he supported in the United States and in nations that he persuaded to follow his lead in support of homosexuality. An example of political leaders causing the people of the land to suffer is when there was a famine in the days of King David. When David prayed to God, the Lord told him that the famine was for the sins of his predecessor King Saul (2 Sam. 21:1). The nation also suffered for the sins of King Manasseh (2 Kings 21:10–16). David himself made an unwise political decision when he ordered a census against God's will, and that caused 70,000 people to die by the hand of God and his holy angel (1 Chron. 21:14–17). Just as King Jeroboam caused Israel to stop following the Lord and made them sin a great sin, Pres. Barack Obama and other anti-God politicians assisted in doing the same thing in America and in the entire world (2 Kings 17:21). So, leaders do indeed cause us to suffer by the hand of God because of their decisions and actions against God. The endorsement of homosexual marriage by President Obama and other world leaders has and will continue to cause suffering in the world. God says, "Shall I not visit for these things? Shall not my soul be avenged on such a nation?" (Jer. 5:9; 29; 14:10).

What we have come to know as Hurricane Katrina was the result of a sinful nation, so was 9/11, but not everyone who died in those tragedies were lost (Luke 13:1–5). The Bible describes our society in the following scripture:

> God is just in all that is brought upon us, for God has done right, but we have done wickedly. Neither have our kings [presidents and politicians] kept God's law, nor hearkened or obeyed God's commandments and God's testimonies. For they have not served God in their kingdom [nation], in the large and fat land which God gave them, neither did they turn from their wicked works. (Neh. 9:33–35)

God said concerning the nation of Babylon and heathens, "As she has done, do unto her" (Jer. 50:15; 29; Obad. 15). Nations, like people, reap what they sow. Blessed is the nation whose God is the Lord (Ps. 33:12). In every nation, people who fear Christ and work righteousness are accepted by Christ (Acts 10:35). God has mercy on people who fear him (Luke 1:50). God's wrath toward us is according to our fear toward him (Ps. 90:11). Therefore, when people are bold in their support of sin, including homosexuality, and of other sins, God's wrath is harder because people stood hard against him (Ps. 90:11).

Evil law officials try to corrupt and make God's Word void. Therefore, according to Ps. 119:126, it is time for God to work, as he did on September 11, 2001. God causes all people to stop working so that he can do his own work (Job 37:7). Again, not everyone who died on 9/11 was lost (Luke 13:1–5). But on that day, God had a controversy with the people of the land, because there "is" no truth, no mercy, nor knowledge of God (Hosea 4:1–2). For example, shortly before 9/11, courts in the United States allowed executions to be seen live on television and some gays received the right to marry and to adopt children.

Disobedience to God can also cause wars. The Bible says, "The eyes of the Lord run throughout the whole earth; to show himself strong on behalf of people whose heart is perfect toward him. But you have done foolishly, therefore from now on you shall have wars" (2 Chron. 16:9). The eyes of the Lord are over righteous people, and his ears are open unto their prayers, but the face of the Lord is against people who do evil (1 Pet. 3:12).

As stated earlier, God says that if "his people" who are called by "his name" shall humble themselves and pray and seek his face and turn from their wicked ways, then will he hear from heaven and heal the nation (2 Chron. 7:14; Matt. 13:15; Luke 19:37–42). God did not say if sinners obey him, but he said if people who are called by Christ's name shall obey him. The judgment of God starts at the church, with God's people (1 Pet. 4:17). It is the weak, hypocritical, straddling the fence, two-faced, double-standard, hard-hearted, and backsliding Christians who are preventing God from healing the land.

God says that we must obey kings, presidents, politicians, and leaders with singleness of heart but only if those leaders have laws according to God's Word and to stand for God's Word is to not be doubled-minded, double-tongued, or doublehearted (2 Chron. 30:12; James 1:5–8; 1 Tim. 3:8; 1 Chron. 12:8, 33, 35, 37–38; Ps. 12:1–4; Eccles. 5:8).

Most Christians who support gay marriage do not even want their own children to be gay. How hypocritical is that? Christians of any nation must not support the sinful laws of that land. Even if they cannot prevent it, they must not support it or speak in favor of it. Otherwise, their ways will cause their nation to reap what Christians helped it to sow. When any nation keeps the law of the land aligned with God's Word, they are a blessed nation that lives by the following scripture:

> "I have taught you statutes and judgments, even as the Lord my God commanded me. Keep therefore and do them, for this is your wisdom and understanding in the sight of the nations. For what nation is so great, who has God so near unto them,

as the Lord our God is in all things that we call upon him for? And what nation is there so great, that has statutes and judgments so righteous? Teach them to your children, and to your grandchildren." (Deut. 4:5–9; Jer. 32:37–44)

CHRISTIANS WHO SUPPORT GAYS ARE CALLING GOD A LIAR

The New Testament scripture that says homosexuality is not allowed states that supporters of homosexuality have changed the truth of God into a lie (Rom. 1:24–28). The Holy Scripture also says, "Let God be true and every human a liar...that you may overcome when you are judged by God, because if our sins showed how righteous God is, would it be unrighteous for God to punish us? No, because if it was wrong for God to punish us, how would he judge the world?" (Rom. 3:3–6). If we confess our sins, admit that homosexuality and other sin is wrong and that God is right, God is faithful to forgive our sins and cleanse us from all unrighteousness, but if we say that any sin in the Bible is not sin, we call God a liar, and the truth is not in us (1 John 1:9–10). If a person robs their father or mother and says that it is not sin, God says that sinner is even worse when they say that they are not wrong for robbing their parents (Prov. 28:24). The same applies to homosexuals who say they are not wrong for being gay.

Concerning changing the truth of God into a lie, "Our transgressions have multiplied before God, and we know our sins. We lie against the Lord, and depart away from our God, speaking from the heart words of falsehood. Yes, truth fails, and they who depart from evil are attacked and persecuted, and it displeases the Lord that there is such evil judgment in the courts" (Isa. 59:12–15).

When people tell lies to glorify God, that only makes them a bigger sinner, and God does not want glory that comes from a lie (Rom. 3:7). People who say it is all right to do something that is contrary to the Holy Scripture are saying that God is like them, but the Lord will set things in order (Ps. 50:21). God says a liar shall not dwell in his sight (Ps. 101:7). Some people struggle with and twist, neglect, and reject scriptures to their own destruction (2 Pet. 3:15–18). The Bible says that whoever shall add or take away from the Word of God shall be taken out of the Book of Life, and if we do add to God's Word, he will reprove us and we shall be found a liar (Deut. 4:2; 12:32; Ezra 6:11; Prov. 30:5–6; Eccles. 3:14–15; Rom. 1:24, 25; Rev. 22:18–19; 2 Pet. 3:16).

The Bible says that Jesus died for the sins of the whole world, but it goes on to say that we know him when we consistently obey him and people who say they know Christ without obeying him is a liar (John 6:51; 11:47–52; 1 John 2:2–4; Acts 17:26; Heb. 2:9; Rom. 5:6–9; 8:32; Isa. 53; 1 Tim. 2:1–7).

John the Baptist said that Christ is the Lamb of God who takes away the sin of the world, after we repent for our sins (John 1:29). John also said that Christ must increase and that we must decrease (John 3:28, 30–31). So, Christ was offered once to bear the sins of many. To people who eagerly wait for Christ, he will appear a second time not to deal with sin, but to bring salvation to people who have obeyed his Word and waited patiently for his return (Heb. 9:28). The Bible says that Jesus is the Savior of all people, especially of people who believe (1 Tim. 4:10; John 11:47–52).

Therefore, people who do not believe, or believe and do not obey, are very much likely not to be saved (Mark 16:16; John 3:3–7; Acts 5:32).

The Lord says he is tired of people saying everyone who sins is good in the sight of the Lord and that he delights in them (Mal. 2:17). Sure, he loves everyone, but he does not delight in everyone or every action (Deut. 10:17–22). The same applies with us toward our kids. We love them, but we do not support certain things that they do. People who disregard the Word of God praise the wicked, but they who keep the Word of God contends with the wicked (Prov. 28:4). We are to have no fellowship or relations with the unfruitful works of darkness, but rather rebuke them (Eph. 5:11). "Let no one deceive you with vain words. These things cause the wrath of God upon the children of disobedience. Be not partakers with them. The fruit of the Spirit is goodness, righteousness, and truth. Proving what is acceptable unto the Lord" (Eph. 5:6–12; Rom. 12:1–2).

God is a loving, merciful, and gracious God but some of those same scriptures also say within the same text that God is sometimes a terrible God when he punishes people for their sins (Exod. 34:10; Deut. 7:21; 10:17; Neh. 1:5; 4:14; 9:32; Job 37:22; Ps. 47:2; Jer. 20:11).

ADOPTION OF CHILDREN BY GAY PEOPLE SHOULD NOT BE ALLOWED

Equity or fairness according to God is different from what mankind may consider equity to be because God says we must have equity but only while standing for the Word of God (Isa. 59:14). If human's idea of equity is to water down or disregard the Bible, that equity must not be provided, as in the case of two gay people adopting children or getting married (Isa. 59:14). It is impossible for gay people to biologically produce children, so the truth is that it should be impossible for them to be granted the equity that heterosexual couples have regarding adopting children and marrying each other.

As with some heterosexual couples, when a gay couple adopts a child, that child could be in danger of being sexually abused, not to mention the fact that they could be mocked and teased by their peers. And when the adopted kids are adopted as babies, they have no choice as to whether they want to have gay parents. When gay people adopt children, red flags are already obvious because they have admitted that they have a perverted lifestyle.

The Bible says to train up a child in the way they should go, and when they are old, they will not depart from it (Prov. 22:6). When children are raised by two twisted and perverted people that think that they are normal parents, the child may not know the right way when they are old. Some children will be gay at a young age by choice, and some will grow up to be gay by choice when they become adults, but when the president of the United States and leaders of certain other nations endorsed homosexuality, that caused some children who would not have been gay to become gay because the leader of the nation said it is all right for gays to marry and to adopt children. If God wanted two people of the same sex to raise children, he would have made it possible for them to sexually produce children. This proves that homosexuality is evil, because no matter how many times they have sex, they still cannot produce children.

MUSLIMS DO NOT SUPPORT GAY LIFESTYLES AS MUCH AS HYPOCRITE CHRISTIANS DO

When hypocrite Christians support homosexuality or are homosexuals themselves, they are setting a bad example for non-Christians like Muslims who some Christians say are bad people, when actually some Christians are worse than Muslims in a lot of ways, including in their support of homosexuality (Jer. 2:33). Pres. Barack Obama was probably a Muslim who claimed to be a Christian to win the presidency of the United States, but if he was indeed a Muslim, he was not a very good one because Muslims do not support homosexuality as much as so-called Christians do.

The gay rights movement that started in the early 2000s was led by mostly American and European nations, which are mostly white people who claim to be Christians. But those American and European nations are more hypocritical, evil, anti-God, and antichrist than the so-called anti-God nations of Africa and Asia who do not embrace Christ as much but still know better than to support homosexuality. The Bible highlights situations like that when people who confess Christ are actually worse than people who do not confess Christ (Jer. 2:32–33; 5:28–31; 2 Chron. 33:9; Matt. 5:19; 23:15; 2 Kings 21:10–12; Lam. 4:6; Ezek. 16:47–48; 23:1–11; Judg. 19:11–30; 20:1–14; 1 Tim. 5:8; 1 Cor. 5:1–6).

In the following scriptures, God lists the sins that other nations were committing, and he commanded that we be holy, not like them, and separated unto him and from sinners (Lev. 20). The part of those scriptures that say people would be put to death for their sins has been voided by the death of Christ, but death still eventually happens to sinners, because the wages of sin is death (Rom. 1:18–32; 6:23; 1:18–32; 2 Thess. 2:10–15; 8:13–14; 1 Kings 13:11–24; 1 Cor. 11:23–30; Ezek. 7:13; 18:4; 33:11; 19–20; Deut. 30:19–20; Job 20:11; 24:19; 36:5–13; Ps. 1:5–6; Prov. 19:5, 9; 21:16; 27:20; 30:15, 16; Isa. 5:14; 13:9; Josh. 7:1–13; 1 Chron. 10:13–14; Rev. 2:23; Matt. 18:11–14; Lam. 3:31–33; 1 Tim. 2:4; 2 Pet. 3:9; Luke 13:1–5).

OBAMA CAUSED PEOPLE TO LIVE BY THE COMMANDMENTS OF MAN

Job was one of the most righteous people to ever live, and he said that destruction from God was a terror to him (Job 1:1, 6–8; 2:1–3; 31:13–23; James 5:10–11).

The Bible says, "Draw near unto God, and he will draw near unto you. Cleanse your hands, you sinners, and purify your hearts, you double-minded" (James 4:8). Any Christian who supported Barack Obama after he endorsed homosexuality is doublehearted. God says in the Old Testament, "People draw near me with their mouth, and honor me with their lips, but have removed their heart far from me, and their fear towards me is taught by the rules of mankind" (Isa. 29:13). They disregarded God's Word and lived by the laws and rules that the anti-God government made (2 Kings 17:19; Ps. 28:4–5). In the New Testament, God says, "People draw near me with their mouth, and honor me with their lips, but their heart is far from me. In vain do they worship me, teaching for doctrines the commandments of mankind" (Mark 7:6–7; Col. 2:22; Titus 1:14; Jer. 12:2; Ezek. 33:31; John 7:18; 1 John 3:18; 1 Thess. 2:4–6, 13).

One of God's Ten Commandments says, "Thou shalt not use the name of the Lord thy God in vain, for the Lord will not hold people guiltless who use his name in vain" (Exod. 20:7). We must obey the Word of God for what it is—the Word of God and not the word of mankind (Eph. 4:14; 1 Cor. 2:9–16; 1 Thess. 2:4–6, 13).

The Book of Malachi says, "You have wearied the Lord with your words. Yet you say, how have we wearied him? When you say everyone who does evil is good in the sight of the Lord, or, where is God?" (Mal. 2:17). People who believe that all they have to do to be saved is confess with their mouth and believe in their heart have mentioned God's name, but not in truth (the whole truth) nor in righteousness (Isa. 48:1; Rom. 10:9–10, 13; Heb. 6:1–6; Luke 4:4; Exod. 24:7; Deut. 4:1–9; 8:3).

When President Obama and others supported and endorsed homosexuality, those were evil commandments of humans, and they thought no evil would come upon them as a form of punishment from God (Mic. 3:11; Ezek. 33:31). Christ also says, "Not everyone who says unto me, Lord, Lord, shall enter into the kingdom of heaven, but they who do the will of my Father in heaven shall go to heaven" (Matt. 7:21–23; Mic. 3:11).

Christ will say to them, "I never knew you. Depart from me, you worker of iniquity" (Matt. 7:21–23; Deut. 32:4–5). Christ shall say to those people, "I never knew you as being holy and sanctified," and then God will shut the door to heaven, just like in the days of Noah when God shut the door to the ark when he destroyed the earth with water (Luke 13:24–27; Matt. 7:21–23; Exod. 33:17). Thus, some people claim to be Christians but are sinners, and they think that God is with them and that he will not punish them or allow trouble to come into their lives (Mic. 3:11).

SOME PEOPLE IDOLIZED OBAMA AND HE WAS ALREADY AN ANTICHRIST

The Bible also says that even though the Lord is high, he considers the lowly, but the proud he knows afar off (Ps. 138:6). Job was upright before God, feared God, and despised evil and sin (Job 1:1). Shouldn't we all try to be like Christ, like Job, and like other righteous men and women in the Bible (Job 24:1–11, 29, 31)?

Sometimes God puts the basest of people over an entire nation (Dan. 4:17, 25, 32; 5:21; Jer. 27:4–13). Just as he allowed Barack Obama to be president even though Obama was never a good Christian. God used Cyrus, Nebuchadnezzar, and an Egyptian pharaoh to do his will; and he even called two of those men his servants, even though they did not know God and did not serve him in holiness; but without holiness, no one can see God (2 Chron. 36:22–23; Ezra 6:1–5; Isa. 44:28; 45:1–10; Jer. 25:1–12; 27:1–13; 29:1–14; 43:10; Dan. 4:24–37; Rom. 9:17; Heb. 12:14–15; 1 Pet. 1:14–16; 1 Tim. 2:8).

If any Christian is opposed to this message because it speaks against Pres. Barack Obama, they must understand that when he spoke against God's Word, he blasphemed against God, and he was a version of the antichrist (Matt. 12:31–32; 1 John 2:18).

So, it is very appropriate for Christians to speak against Obama, but for Christians to support him and defend him is to make him their idol, which means they are guilty of idolatry, because they put Obama above God (Acts 4:19). What if President Obama had said that he did not believe that Christ rose from the dead? Hopefully all Christians would have forsaken and abandoned Obama for saying that. It is the same when he said that it is all right for gays to marry. At that time, Obama basically said, God *is not*. When the leader of anything supports, endorses, or embraces something or someone, some of the population will be influenced to follow their lead, even causing some children to grow up in sin and perverseness. And that is exactly what Obama did.

So, all Christians should forsake President Obama because he blasphemed God. Any Christian who cannot understand this has serious issues and should look in the mirror and, in their hearts, where they claim Christ is, because Mr. Obama is in their heart too. That is why they cannot let go of their support of him. Obama cursed God when he endorsed gay marriage. Christians who cannot forsake President Obama are also cursing God.

Mr. Obama never included the name of Christ, Bible scripture, or anything from the Bible in his Christmas cards, because he was *antichrist*. Obama cursed God when he endorsed gay marriage. Christians who cannot forsake President Obama are also cursing God.

While Job was suffering near unto death, his wife told him to curse God and die so his suffering could end, but Job refused and said to his wife and friends, "Though God slay me, yet I still trust in God" (Job 2:8–10; 13:15–16). Notice that God took the life of Job's children after Job prayed regularly for his children's safety (Job 1:1–5). Christians often brag about how righteous Job was, and we all should want to be like Job. But Job would not have supported gay marriage because he despised sin and refused to deny God, or to forsake God, or to curse God, or to blaspheme God even though God allowed him to suffer the loss of all his children, most of his wealth, and his health (Job 1:1; 2:9–10). But Christians who support homosexuality are cursing God to his face, because they are saying God is wrong and they are right. God's Word says homosexuality is not allowed and is against God's will (Rom. 1:24–28; 1 Cor. 6:9; Lev. 18:22; 20:13).

Again, we must not partially obey God's Word, but we must try to obey all of it (1 Tim. 5:20–21; Luke 4:4; Exod. 24:7; Deut. 4:1–9; 8:3).

To those of you who are truly sanctified and will never deny Christ, Revelations 3:8 reads, "I know your works, behold, I have set before you an open door, and no one can shut it. For you have a little strength, and have kept my Word, and have not denied my name," as was the case with Job (Job 13:15–16).

The Apostle James asked, "Why do we favor rich people when a lot of them blaspheme the name of Jesus whose name we claim that we wear and confess?" (James 2:1–7). President Obama was very intelligent and educated, he was powerful, and he was rich. But the Bible says, "Let not the intelligent and educated boast in their intelligence, let not the powerful boast in their power, and let not the rich boast in their riches. But let people who boast, boast in this, that they understand and know me, that I am the Lord who exercises loving-kindness, judgment, and righteousness in the earth. For in these things do I delight, says the Lord" (Jer. 9:23–24). But they who boast, let them boast in the Lord, for they who commend themselves are not approved by God, but people who God commends are approved (2 Cor. 10:17–18). We must seek honor from God alone and not from each other (John 5:41, 44; 7:18; 12:43; 2 Cor. 3:1–4; 1 Thess. 2:4–6).

The Bible says that people who are in honor but do not understand God are like the beasts that perish (Ps. 49:16–20).

Some versions of the Bible erroneously change those scriptures indicating that it is all right to seek honor from mankind, but when you seek honor from only God by serving him in holiness, you will automatically eventually receive honor from humans too.

There are only a few sanctified and real Christians, but there are more than it appears to the naked eye. Jeremiah was jealous for the Lord when it seemed like everyone forsook the Lord except him. God's and Jeremiah's conversation was as thus, "I have been very jealous for the Lord, because the children of Israel have forsaken the covenant, and I, even I only, am remained, and they seek my life, to take it away." But God told Jeremiah, "Yet I have seven thousand true servants in Israel who have not bowed to Baal and have not kissed his face" (1 Kings 19:15–18; Rom. 11:1–5; 1 Kings 18:26–32; Deut. 5:9).

Baal was an idol god, and President Obama is an idol god to people who supported him after he blasphemed Christ by approving gay marriage and the adoption of children by gay people.

OBAMA DID SOME SHORT-TERM GOOD BUT MORE LONG-TERM HARM

There are many good people in the world, but when Christ says that no one is good but the Father in heaven, he means that no one is as good, gracious, and merciful as God and that no matter what good a person does on earth, their goodness does not mean anything to the Father if they do other things against God (Matt. 19:17). And the legalization of gay marriages will be almost impossible for mankind to reverse, and that is why Barack Obama did more long-term harm than he did short-term good when he did indeed assist people with short-term benefits. Therefore, it does not matter how much good President Obama did, because even the devil makes himself appear to be good and a minister of light and his ministers appear to be ministers of righteousness (2 Cor. 11:13–15). This means Obama appeared to be good because he was a family man and did certain good things in society, but the support of gay marriage and abortions voids all the good that he did. God says that when he forgives us, he forgets all the wrong we did after we truly repent and turn away from sins. But God also says that he forgets all the good that we did after we leave him and do things against his Word (Ezek. 33:10–16).

Jesus tells us to beware of wolves in sheep's clothing, and Christians should have recognized President Obama by the fruits he produced. Mr. Obama's fruits produced words and laws against God (Matt. 7:15–29). The Apostle Paul said that his speech and preaching were not with enticing words of man's wisdom, but in the demonstration of the Spirit and power of God (1 Cor. 2:4, 9–16; Ps. 92:5; 1 Chron. 28:9).

The Apostle Paul also said that if a man or an angel teaches you anything other than what the apostles taught, let it be accused. And there is no other gospel than that of Christ and the apostles.

The United States did not make lynching and hanging a federal crime until the year 2022, which is also a disgrace. The black president Barack Obama did not use the power of his pen to create an anti – lynching law. Barack Obama also failed to make Juneteenth a national holiday. And President Obama did not visit Tulsa, Oklahoma to support descendants of the Tulsa race massacre of 1921. But Joe Biden, a white president, did all these things for black people.

WE MUST BE A LIVING SACRIFICE AFTER CHRIST WAS A CRUCIFIED SACRIFICE

When God sent the Jews into captivity and slavery for not serving him properly, the righteous people and prophets such as Daniel went into captivity with the sinners. Good people suffered with bad people, so the church must be more active in society or Christians could suffer with sinners and with hypocrite Christians (Matt. 13:24– 30, 36–50). Daniel was thrown into the lion's den for not obeying an earthly king (Dan. 6). Shadrach, Meshach, and Abednego were thrown into a fiery furnace for not supporting an idol god and an earthly king when most of God's people did obey the king (Dan. 3). Christians who supported President Obama were the same as the people in the Bible who were not thrown in the fiery furnace but instead honored and supported an anti-God king, but Obama supporters were not even faced with losing their life if they had rejected and forsook President Obama. They instead rejected and forsook God without even being threatened with harm and danger if they opposed Barack Obama and the legalization of gay marriages and the adoption of children by gay couples. But hell is hotter than the fiery furnace (Rev. 20:10). God is commanding all nations to defy and deny supporters of gay marriage and homosexuality altogether like how Shadrach, Meshach, and

Abednego defied and denied the earthly king, choosing to be thrown into the fiery furnace instead (Dan. 3). They said that God Almighty would deliver them, but if not, they would rather die than put God second (Dan. 3:14-18). Hallelujah. Amen.

People during the Old Testament times were not under the current blood and grace of Jesus because he had not been sacrificed yet. But their work was accounted unto them for righteousness, and they will still go to heaven (Gal. 3:6; Heb. 11:13, 39; 1 Pet. 4:6; Rev. 22:10-13; Ps. 106:6-31).

Job and Balaam lived in the Old Testament. And Job said that worms will eat his dead body, but that he knew that his Redeemer lives, and that God will stand on the last day and that he will still see God for himself (Job 19:25-27). Balaam said that he shall see Christ, but not now, and that he still shall see him someday (Num. 24:15-17). Christians must seek a better nation in heaven (Heb. 11:13-16; Phil. 3:20). To God, all nations are nothing, even less than nothing (Isa. 40:17). If you are currently risen with Christ, seek those things that are above, where Christ sits on the right hand of God. Set your affections on things above, not on things of the earth (Col. 3:1-2). The way of life is above to the wise, that they may depart from hell beneath (Prov. 15:24). A scripture in the book of Psalms says, "Who do I have in heaven besides you Lord, and there is none on earth who I desire besides you" (Ps. 73:25). "Seek ye first the kingdom of God, and his righteousness, and your needs and necessities, along with some of your wants and desires shall be added unto you. Where your treasure is, there will your heart be also, whether your treasure is godly or ungodly, or whether your treasure is in heaven or on earth" (Matt. 6:19-21, 24-33; 19:16-30; Rom. 2:6-11; Phil. 2:21; Heb. 11:24-27; 1 Kings 3:7-15).

God told one hardworking man that he would die because the man pursued earthly possessions and was not equally rich toward God (Luke 12:16-21; Isa. 40:21-25). Why is there in the hand of a fool the purchase price of wisdom, since they have no heart for it (Prov. 17:16; 18:1-2)? King Solomon asked God for wisdom instead of riches, long life, and vengeance of his enemies; therefore, God gave him wisdom, rest, and riches and the land God gave peace (1 Kings 3:10–12; 10:21, 27; 1 Chron. 22:9).

People seek their own and not the things that are of Jesus Christ (Phil. 2:21; 1 Tim. 6:9–10; James 3:13–16; John 5:41, 44; 1 Cor. 13:5).

"Know ye not that unrighteousness shall not enter the kingdom of God? Be not deceived, neither fornicators, idolaters, adulterers, homosexuals, thieves, covetous people, drunkards, revilers, nor extortioners shall inherit the kingdom of God" (1 Cor. 6:9–11). God is commanding that we all seek his face and not just his prosperity, protection, grace, and mercy (Ps. 27:8). Otherwise, as stated earlier, God says, "I will go and return to my place until they acknowledge their sins, and seek my face, in their affliction they will seek me early" (Hosea 5:3–6, 15; Ps. 78:34).

The Holy Scripture says that most people have not resisted to blood striving against sin, and most of us will never be faced with dying for Christ to prove our love for him or to prove that we are a true servant of the Lord (Heb. 12:4; James 4:7; John 17:14–19; 1 Cor. 10:8–13).

If we never have to die for the Lord, we can at least be a living sacrifice, holy, acceptable unto God, not conformed to this world, but transformed by the renewing of our mind (Rom. 12:1–2; 2 Tim. 2:15).

OBAMA WAS NOT THE ONLY ANTI-GOD PRESIDENT

Some supporters of Pres. Barack Obama said that certain presidents before and after Barack Obama were not saved, sanctified, holy, or godly Christians either and that both former president George H. W. Bush and his son former president George W. Bush started wars and caused death and suffering. That is indeed true, but Christ says there will be wars and rumors of wars (Matt. 24:6). So we do not know if God started those wars or not, and Moses said that God is a God of war (Exod. 15:3). But we do know that God did not speak through President Obama to cause him to say that it is all right for gays to marry, because God cannot lie and has never lied (Titus 1:2; Heb. 6:18; Jer. 15:15–21; Ezek. 33:33; Ps. 89:30–37).

Some wars were started by God to punish people for their sins. The Israelites fought several battles on the way to the promised land and after entering the promised land (Exod. 17:11–13). Thus, Moses, Joshua, Caleb, and certain others were sometimes army generals (Num. 31:3–4; Josh. 11:16–23; 2 Kings 13:25).

And the prophets Elisha and Samuel were instructed by God to kill heathen enemies of God's people, but since the death and resurrection of Christ who died to allow everyone time to repent, including homosexuals, God does not want humans to kill other humans (1 Sam. 15:33; 1 Kings 19:15–18).

Real Christians do nothing against the truth, but for the truth (2 Cor. 13:8). God is perfect, right, just, true, and without sin (Deut. 32:4; Ps. 18:30; 92:15; Heb. 2:16–18; 4:15; Gal. 2:17).

GAYS SHOULD NOT EXPECT GOD TO THINK LIKE THEM

God himself says to people who lie to glorify the Lord, or lie to justify themselves, "Let God be truth and everyone else a liar" (Rom. 3:4-8), because God is not like us, and we cannot expect him to change his ways to accommodate or support our filthy sins (Ps. 50:21; Isa. 55:8-9). The Lord says, "My thoughts are not your thoughts, nor are your ways my ways. For as the heavens are higher than the earth, so are my ways and my thoughts higher than your ways and your thoughts" (Isa. 55:8-9; Ps. 50:16-23; 92:5).

God says that he often keeps silent when people sin, and some people think that God is like them, but he will punish them and put things in order (Ps. 50:21-23). Job said that what we do know about God is only some of God's ways (Job 26). And the New Testament tells us that God's ways are past finding out (Rom. 11:33). God is burdened and wearied with people and the sins that they insist he accepts (Isa. 43:24). God's ways and thoughts are much deeper and higher than ours, and we must seek and search his Word, his ways, his thoughts, and his righteousness (1 Cor. 1:10; 2:9-16; Rom. 15:5-6). God cannot be worshipped with human hands because he does not need anything, but God must be worshipped in spirit and in truth (John 4:23-24; Acts 17:25).

God says regarding the enemies of Christian people, "Many

people have gathered against you, but they do not know the thoughts of the Lord, nor do they understand his counsel, for he shall destroy them. All people walk in the name of their god, and we in the name of the Lord our God forever, and ever" (Mic. 4:12). Wicked people, through pride, will not seek God, because God is not in their thoughts (Ps. 10:4). The anger of the Lord shall not return until he has executed and until he has performed the thoughts of his heart. In the latter days, you will consider it perfectly (Jer. 23:20). God will not uphold a sin, but the Lord will punish his enemies and they who go on still in their sins (Ps. 68:21; 78:32).

God and his Word have always been and will continue to be the same, and he does not change for anyone (Ps. 102:25–28; 119:89–96; 147:5; Eccles. 3:14–15; Heb. 1:10–12; 13:8–9).

The merciful part of God's Word has not changed either (Mal. 3:5–7). God does not change, and if he did, we all would already be dead because of our sins, but he sent his Son Jesus to die for us until we repent (Mal. 3:6–7; Heb. 10:26–31; Exod. 20:18, 19; Deut. 5:23–26).

God's Word also says that some people fall short of his grace and mercy because of sin (Heb. 3:7–19; 4:1). The Bible says, "Let them who think they stand take heed or they will fall too" (1 Cor. 10:1–14).

IT IS BLASPHEMOUS TO SAY THAT CHRIST AND THE APOSTLES WERE GAY

The Bible talks about the disciple who Christ loved. That disciple often sat near Christ and hugged him, but they certainly were not gay (John 21:7, 20–25). Christ considers all his saved and sanctified true and faithful servants to be his spiritual spouses (Rev. 19:7; 21:2, 9).

Someone on the radio once said that Christ was gay, but he certainly was not, and Christ was a virgin (Heb. 2:16–18; 4:14–16; Num. 23:19; 1 John 3:5; Ps. 18:30; 92:15; 1 Pet. 2:21–23; Gal. 2:17).

The Apostle Paul in the King James Version of the New Testament told his followers that he espoused them to one husband, that one husband being Christ, and that he may present them as a chaste virgin to Christ (2 Cor. 11:2; Col. 1:27–28).

David and Jonathan were the best of friends, and when Johnathan died, David said that Jonathan's friendship surpassed the love of women (2 Sam. 1:17, 26). But they were not gay. When God called David to be king, David was chosen after God's own heart, and if David had been gay, that would not have been after God's own heart, and God would not have chosen David to be king (1 Sam. 13:14; Acts 13:21–24).

David also said that the Word of God is settled in heaven forever and will not change and that he would have perished if the Word of God had not been his delight (Ps. 119:89–96). And the Word of God says that homosexuality is forbidden by God, and that Word is settled in heaven (Rom. 1:24–28; 1 Cor. 6:9; Lev. 18:22; 20:13).

GOD'S PUNISHMENT NOWADAYS IS HARDER THAN THAT OF SODOM AND GOMORRAH IN THE PAST

In the Old Testament, sinners died at the hands of human judges, but the judgment of God shall be worse, because homosexuals and their supporters have trodden underfoot the Son of God and counted his blood an unholy thing, and they do it despite of the Spirit of grace. Thus, "Vengeance is mine, I will repay, says the Lord" (Heb. 10:26–31; Exod. 20:18–19; Rom. 12:19–21; Nah. 1:1–3; Ps. 94; 1 Sam. 25:2–39; Deut. 2; 25:17–19; 32:35–43).

God says that he will have vengeance on people who do not know God and on people who do not obey the gospel and Word of our Lord and Savior Jesus Christ. They shall be punished with everlasting destruction and flaming fire (2 Thess. 1:7–9).

The Lord shall judge his people. "Woe unto them who call evil good and good evil" (Isa. 5:20–25; 13:6–13; Rom. 3:4–8). "It is a fearful thing to fall into the hands of the living God" (Heb.

10:26–31; Exod. 20:18–19; Deut. 5:23–26).

Christ says that the people of Sodom and Gomorrah had a better chance of surviving than gays and other sinners nowadays (Matt. 10:14–15). Thus, the destruction of Sodom and Gomorrah and of the Israelites in the wilderness after slavery in Egypt is an example to everyone who lives ungodly nowadays (2 Pet. 2:4–6; Jude 1:5–7). And the life of Christ is an example of how we should live nowadays (1 Pet. 2:21).

To people who say the destruction of Sodom and Gomorrah happened a long time ago, and that God does not do things like that anymore, or that God has never truly destroyed a place like that before, well, even in this century, God has killed hundreds of thousands of people at once in certain cities and nations around the world. We do not know how many people died in Sodom and Gomorrah, but it is highly possible that more people died when God sent destructive wars and weather recently than when Sodom and Gomorrah were destroyed. The only difference is that God has not destroyed whole cities and whole nations lately, but due to sin, he has and will continue to destroy thousands of people at a time until he returns on judgment day (2 Tim. 3:1–7; Jer. 5:10).

Christ says that an evil and adulterous generation seeks after a sign and that the only sign given to this generation is the sign of Jonah in the belly of the whale for three days and three nights, but a greater sign than Jonah is here now, and that is Christ, who has all power (Matt. 28:18; 1 Cor. 15:24–28; Eph. 1:21–23; Col. 2:10; Phil. 2:9; Ps. 8; Heb. 2:5–9; John 16:15).

Christ was in the grave for three days and three nights. Jonah was in the dark whale's stomach, but Christ was beaten with whips and stones, stabbed with a spear, and nailed to the cross with huge nails and then was placed dead in a dark cold grave. A greater sign than Jonah is here now, and if our nations do not repent as Nineveh did who made even their animals fast with them, a greater destruction will occur too (Matt. 12:39–42).

Sodom and Gomorrah were bad, but these times are worse, and Jesus says that if they had seen the works, blessings, grace, and mercy that he is shining on our generation, then even Sodom would have repented (Matt. 11:20–24). Jesus also says that New Testament times are only the beginning of sorrows (Matt. 24:8). The New Testament is still a better testament (Heb. 7:22). Israel was so bad at one point that God punished them worse than Sodom (Lam. 4:6). But the punishment on our generation will be and is at times the worst ever. As stated earlier, Christ says that this is an evil, adulterous, and demonic generation (Dan. 12:1 – 3; Matt. 12:39–45). And demons do not always reveal themselves as evil, but as wolves who look like sheep and as angels who are really devils (Matt. 7:15–29; 2 Cor. 11:14–15).

The sins of the people of Sodom and Gomorrah were before God exceedingly (Gen. 13:13). Willful and habitual sins including homosexuality are before God nowadays, and this generation is worse than the generation of Sodom and Gomorrah. The Bible says, "Their tongue and their doings are against the Lord, to provoke the eyes of his glory. The show of their appearance does witness against them; and they declare their sin as Sodom; they hid it not. Woe unto their soul! For they have rewarded evil unto themselves" (Isa. 3:8–11; 13:11). They glorify in what should be their shame, and they shall self – destruct because they are enemies of the cross of Christ," (Phil. 3:16–21). God says further, "I will punish the world for their evil and the wicked for their iniquity, and I will cause the arrogance of proud people to cease and will lay low the haughtiness of the terrible" (Isa. 13:11). At another point, God told the people of Jerusalem, "I will wipe Jerusalem as a person wipes a dish, wiping it and turning it upside down" (2 Kings 21:13). In yet another scripture, God says, "As they gather silver, brass, iron, and tin into the furnace to melt it, so will I gather you in my anger and in my fury, and I will leave you there and melt you" (Ezek. 22:20–22).

Although our generations are the worst ever, we receive the slowest and most delayed punishment ever, but people nowadays neglect the grace that Jesus bought, and neglect causes people of this generation to be punished terribly (Dan. 12:1 – 3; 1 Cor. 6:20; 7:23; 2 Pet. 2:1; Heb. 2:1–3; Matt. 11:20–24).

Some people may say that Christians have been saying for years that these are the last days (2 Pet. 3:3–4, 9–10; Ezek. 8:12; 9:9; Jer. 12:4; 16:17–18; Isa. 40:27; Ps. 94:1–11).

The last days started when John started preaching repentance and to seek the kingdom of heaven (Luke 16:16). These are the latter part of the last days. These last generations have the most ungodly people worldwide than ever before (Matt. 12:39; 16:4; 23:29–33; Mark 8:38; Eph. 5:15–21; Hosea 7:1–4; Phil. 2:15).

PEOPLE HAVE REPROBATE MINDS AND ARE SPIRITUALLY BLIND WHO SUPPORT GAYS

Gays, lesbians, transgenders, bisexuals, and their supporters have reprobate minds, along with other certain sinners who are not gay, and are headed to hell unless they repent, according to the Bible (Rom. 1:18–32; 2 Thess. 2:10–15; 8:13–14; 1 Pet. 2:6–8; 2 Tim. 3:1–8; Titus 1:16; 2 Pet. 2:1–9; Ps. 81:10–12, 15).

People who approve and support gays are also worthy of death (Rom. 1:32). God also points out that people who have reprobate minds will also suffer in the body while they are alive (Rom. 1:27). Reprobate people are blinded by God from the truth, because they insist on living in sin, or they know the truth and still do not care to obey God (Isa. 6:8–13; 29:9–14; Eph. 4:17–32; 2 Cor. 4:3–4; Mark 4:22–25; John 12:37–43; Jer. 13:15–17; Amos 8:11–13; Deut. 29:2–6).

God told the Prophet Isaiah, "I will bring the blind by a way that they knew not. I will lead them in paths that they have not known. I will make darkness light before them, and crooked things straight and not forsake them. They shall be turned back and greatly ashamed who trust in other gods. Hear you deaf and look, you blind, that you may see. Who is blind as my servants and messengers? Seeing many things, but they do not observe, and opening the ears, but they do not hear" (Isa. 42:16–21; 54:4–10).

The same applies to some educated people (Isa. 29:11). Christ referred to another scripture from the book of Isaiah when he said that he speaks to people in parables to give them an example of what he is teaching them, because some people have grown tired of hearing the Word of God and they have closed their eyes, preventing themselves from being healed and delivered (Matt. 13:10–17; Isa. 6:8–13; 29:9–14; Deut. 29:2–6).

PEOPLE ARE NOT JUDGING WHEN THEY QUOTE THE BIBLE IN DEFENSE OF GOD

The Bible says that the Word of God is good if it is used righteously and that it is not made for a righteous person, but for the disobedient, ungodly, sinners, unholy, profane, murderers, whoremongers, homosexuals, people who commit obscene sex acts, kidnappers, slave owners, liars, and any other thing that is contrary to sound doctrine (1 Tim. 1:8–10; Matt. 9:13; Luke 15:2–7).

So-called Christians who support homosexuality twist and corrupt the Word of God (2 Cor. 2:17). If anyone strives for spiritual masteries, they are not crowned unless they strive lawfully (2 Tim. 2:5).

One difference between homosexual relationships and non – homosexual fornication and adultery is that it is easier after repentance to correct a nongay relationship. For example, a fornicating heterosexual couple would have to repent and marry. But the homosexual couple would have a greater challenge of changing and of being perceived as no longer being gay after they repent. Also, although fornication and especially adultery, which is worse than fornication, are both sins just as homosexuality is a sin, fornication and adultery are not abominations; but homosexuality is an abomination, which is a worse sin.

GAYS ARE SOMETIMES POSSESSED WITH A DEMON

There is no such thing as a person being born gay. People choose to be gay on their own, or they are molested and trained or deceived into being gay, or they have an evil spirit dwelling inside of them. When a man says that he feels like he is a woman trapped inside a man's body, and vice versa, that is a demon inside of the body making them feel that way, or they are mentally ill (Matt. 12:43–45; Luke 8:27–34; Acts 19:11–21).

The Bible says, "In the latter days some people shall depart from the faith, giving heed to seducing spirits [demons] and doctrines of devils, speaking lies in hypocrisy" (1 Tim. 4:1–2). Jesus was accused of having a demon in him, but he made it clear that he did not have a demon at all (John 7:19–20; 8:48–52; 14:30). But a devil went into Judas before he betrayed Jesus (Luke 22:1–5; John 6:70; 13:2). People who are not filled with the Holy Ghost are either empty or full of the devil. Jesus was full of the Holy Ghost and not full of the devil (Luke 4:1; John 10:38; 14:30). The Holy Ghost—also called the Holy Spirit—helped Christ to resist the temptations of the devil (Luke 4:1–13). When a person kills someone, performs homosexual acts, or molests a child, people say, "How could they have done that?" Any person who is not full of the Holy Ghost could be capable of doing any evil thing and any sinful thing, because they are empty of the Holy Spirit or full of demons.

The devil is roaming the earth seeking whom he may devour (1 Pet. 5:8; Rev. 12:7–17; Job 1; 2:1–10; 3:16–22; 13:15–16; 42:11).

But as stated earlier, the eyes of the Lord run to and fro throughout the whole earth to show himself strong on behalf of people whose heart is loyal to him (2 Chron. 16:7–10). When the devil crosses your path and you are filled with the Holy Ghost, he is powerless. But if you are not filled with the Holy Spirit, you are in jeopardy. When God cleans us up from sin, our souls are empty until we receive the Holy Spirit inside our body.

Young people are also empty until they are born again through baptism in water in Christ's name (John 3:1–7; Acts 2:36–39; 8:14–17; 10:47–48; 19:2–5).

If we do not receive the Holy Ghost, the devil returns to find us empty and brings seven more demons with him. If you had one evil spirit, now you have eight. If you had five demons, now you have forty. Thus, you become worse than you were before, and the Bible says that this is the same as a dog returning to eat its own vomit (Matt. 12:43–45; 2 Pet. 2:19–22; John 5:14; Lam. 1:8, 9).

Just as when a farmer breaks up fallow ground, he or she must fill it with something, or the weeds will grow worse than before. The same applies to a person's empty soul (Jer. 4:3; Hosea 10:12; Matt. 13:1–23).

All sin is of the devil (1 John 3:8–10; Rom. 6:23; 8:9; John 8:42–47; Ps. 81:10–16). Even cocaine addiction and alcohol addiction are evil spirits and not the Holy Spirit, just as when a person had an evil spirit of deaf and dumb in the Bible and a spirit of sickness (Mark 9:17–25; Luke 11:14; 13:11).

There is also a spirit of the fear of God, of meekness, quietness, wisdom, knowledge, understanding, jealousy, sadness, and the spirit of antichrist and demonic and foul spirits (Num. 5:14, 30; Deut. 34:9; Isa. 11:1–5; Matt. 5:3; Gal. 6:1; Eph. 1:17; 1 Pet. 3:4; 1 John 4:3; Rev. 18:1–2).

Jesus said that he did nothing of himself, but he did only what he saw his Father do (John 5:19). Christ says that he speaks that which he has seen in his Father, and sinners and so-called Christians who do not love the whole truth do those things that they have seen in their father, the devil, and the lusts of the devil they will do, because they are of the devil and are not of God (John 8:34–47; 1 Tim. 5:15). It is also written in another chapter of the Bible, "They who sin are of the devil" (1 John 3:5–10).

When anything in the world is done by humans, either God did it or allowed it, you did it, someone else did it, or the devil did it (Deut. 32:39; John 15:5; 1 Pet. 5:8; Rev. 12:7–17; Job 1; 2; 5:6–7, 17–19; 2 Cor. 2:10–11; Eccles. 8:14).

DRAG QUEENS AND CROSS-DRESSERS

Drag queens and *cross-dressers* are also abominations, even if they are not gay, because it is a sin to wear the clothes of the opposite gender (Deut. 22:5). A person of one sex should not wear the clothes that are strictly made to be worn by the opposite sex, like a man wearing panties or a dress, or a woman dressing in a man's suit or a man's underwear. But God says that workers of abomination will go to hell along with liars, murderers, unbelievers, sorcerers, idolaters, and heterosexuals who commit immoral sex acts; and to be a drag queen or a cross-dresser is an abomination (Heb. 13:4–6; Rev. 21:5–8, 27; 22:14–15).

They can still repent and turn from that sin and be saved by God's grace and mercy (Lam. 3:15–26; Mic. 2:1; Ps. 19:12–14; Eph. 2:2–5).

But God must not be tempted or mocked, nor should his name be used in vain, because we reap what we sow (Gal. 6:7–8; Rom. 2:6; Luke 4:12; 1 Cor. 10:1–12; Exod. 20:7).

HERMAPHRODITES AND INTERSEXUALS

An *intersexual* or *hermaphrodite* is an individual who has both female and male sex organs. The two terms sometimes have different meanings when referenced by some people and by some doctors and scientists. Some people are born with birth defects in the sex organs, just as some people are born with defects in the leg, eye, or brain. That does not mean that God meant for them to be gay. Only one of the sex organs is active and capable of reproducing and conceiving a child. Thus, people born this way are not homosexuals and should not think that they are homosexual. This sometimes happens because of a medical problem during the development of the fetus and could have been allowed by God to punish the parent for their sins, or it could have happened to glorify God when he changes it himself after birth or when he uses the medical profession to change it (John 9:2–3). Besides, can the pottery question what the potter makes? Can we question what God makes? The answer is no (Isa. 45:9–10). God bruises, binds, and wounds but his hands also make people whole (Job 5:18).

TRANSGENDERS, GENDER FLUID, TRANSEXUALS, AND SEX CHANGES

Transgender is appearing or attempting to be a member of the opposite sex, as a *transsexual* or cross-dresser. Some people even go as far to refer to males as she and females as he. Actress and actor Angelina Jolie and Brad Pitt announced that they would allow their kid daughter to identify herself as a boy, which is anti-God. Dwayne Wade and his wife, Gabrielle Union, allowed Wade's son to call himself a girl. Black people looked up to Wade and Union because there are not many black celebrity couples, but Wade and Union, and the Obama's, failed God and were no longer godly examples and role models to an oppressed race of people whose families have been broken and weakened from—as far back as slavery—when children, mothers, fathers, and spouses were separated and sold to other slave masters. It is totally beneficial and vital when, especially young black males, see strong black families as an example of how to raise a family in holiness. Not all black people will agree with these statements, but those black people will erroneously cause themselves to be anti-God if they agree that Wade's male born son should be called a female. Bruce Jenner was given a so-called Courage Award for being transgender, when it was not mostly courage, but mental illness or demonic possession. People and friends who supported Jenner were anti-God and not friends of Christ, but are literally enemies of the cross of Christ (James 4:2-4; John 1:10-12; 15:18-19; 1 John 2:15- 17; 3:13; Rom. 6; 8:1-16; Gal. 5:16-26; 1 Pet. 2:11; 1 Cor. 1:10; 2:9-16; Rom. 15:5-6; Phil. 3:16-21).

The actor Will Smith and his wife the actress Jada Pinkett Smith, and the great former basketball player Magic Johnson are a disgrace and a shame before God and on their black race, because they allowed their sons to choose to pretend to be girls. Lawmakers are right who made it illegal for kids to use hormones that would prevent them from developing as a male in the case of natural born boys, or as a female in the case of natural born girls. This procedure is irreversible, and a person would have to be mentally sick or possessed with a demon to allow their child to permanently change their body from what God made them in their mother's womb (Isa. 45:9-10).

A *transsexual* is a person who has had hormone treatments and surgery to attain the physical characteristics opposite of the sex in which they were born. This too is a sin, because again the clay cannot ask the potter what they are making, and people cannot question how God made them (Isa. 45:9-10). Therefore, *sex changes* are also totally evil. Again, without holiness, no one can see God (Heb. 12:14; Rom. 12:1-2; 2 Tim. 2:15).

"Let us cleanse ourselves from all filthiness of the flesh and spirit, perfecting holiness in the fear of God" (2 Cor. 7:1).

Gender-fluid is relating or pertaining to a person whose gender identity is not fixed and shifts over time or depending on a certain situation. This is truly a case of mental or emotional instability on the part of people who participate in this, and it may even be demonic.

ADULTERY, FORNICATION, AND HOMOSEXUALITY DOES NOT PLEASE GOD

They who are in the flesh cannot please God (Rom. 8:8), because the Spirit is against the flesh and the flesh is against the Spirit (Gal. 5:16-26; 1 Pet. 2:11-12). Flesh and blood cannot inherit the kingdom of heaven but walking and living in the Spirit while you are alive and being changed to a heavenly spirit on judgment day are the only ways to enter heaven (1 Cor. 15:42-52; Gal. 5:16, 24-25; 1 Thess. 4:14-17).

We must be born of the water and of the Spirit, or we cannot go to heaven (John 3:3-7; Acts 2:36-39; 8:14-17; 10:42-48; 19:1-6; Matt. 16:18-19).

Therefore, we must worship God in spirit and in truth and not in the flesh or as a lover of the world (John 4:23-24; Zech. 8:1-8; James 4:2-4; John 1:10-12; 15:18-19; 1 John 2:15-17; 3:13).

When we sow to the flesh, we reap trouble to the flesh, but people who sow to the Spirit shall reap everlasting life in heaven (Gal. 6:7-8). HIV, AIDS, and other sexually transmitted diseases are results of sowing to the flesh, or planting sinful seeds, resulting in reaping pain, and suffering. We must please God, believe that he exists, and diligently seek him (Heb. 11:6)—because if the sinner does not repent, there shall be no reward for them, and their candle shall be put out (Prov. 24:20). To be worldly minded is death, but to be spiritually minded is life and peace, and if anyone does not have the Spirit of God, they do not belong to God (Rom. 8:5–10).

Christ says people act upon what is in their heart and thoughts (Matt. 15:17–20). The Bible also says, "As a person thinks, so are they," even if it is learned behavior (Prov. 23:6–7; Matt. 5:27–29; Ps. 14:1; 53:1; Jer. 17:9–11).

So, be certain you clean yourself of all filthiness of the flesh and spirit, which consists of your inner thoughts and feelings (2 Cor. 7:1; Eph. 4:17–32). If any person does not truly repent, they will lie down in the grave with the sins of their youth (Job 20:11).

In the Old Testament, the Bible says, "You answered them, O Lord God. You were a God who forgave them, though you punished them for their inventions" (Ps. 99:8; Eccles. 7:26–29; Ps. 33:13–15). In the New Testament, God says that people who participate with evil intentions are worthy of death (Rom. 1:21–32). And they will die if they do not repent and live a righteous life, because the consequences and wages of sin is death (Rom. 6:23; Ezek. 7:13; 18:4). Jesus says that he does not know some sinners. That could mean that he does not know them as being holy (Matt. 7:21–23) or that they do not truly know God and could be crooked or perverted (Deut. 32:4–5) or that they do not know God at all (John 15:19–21; 2 John 1:9). Most people know God's blessings, but they do not know the deep things of God (1 Cor. 1:10, 22 – 24; 2:6–16; Ps. 92:5).

Just as a person may know a donation donor but not truly know the donor. And yet to others, the Lord says that although they knew God, they did not glorify him as God (Rom. 1:21). Awake to righteousness and sin not, for some do not know God as well as they think (1 Cor. 15:34; Gal. 4:8–9).

Jesus shall say, "I never knew you," and shut the door to heaven (Luke 13:24–27; Matt. 7:21–23).

HOPE FOR HOMOSEXUALS

As stated before, some people glorify what should be their shame, but they should desire the return of the Savior, and for God to fashion their body like Christ's glorious body (Phil. 3:18–21). The Bible also says that even though the Lord is high, he considers the lowly, but the proud he knows afar off (Ps. 138:6). To uphold homosexuality is to be proud and arrogant. If you have committed homosexual acts in the past, or if you have been raped or molested, that does not mean that you are gay, unless you desire to be that way and keep doing it. You may be ashamed of your past if this is the case. Others may be currently an openly gay person, but when Jesus sets anyone free, they will no longer be a servant of filthy sin (Rom. 6:20–23). They who the Son of God sets free shall be free indeed (John 8:34–36; Rom. 6). Where the Spirit of Christ is, there is freedom (2 Cor. 3:17). But do not use your God-given freedom to sin on occasion (Gal. 5:13), nor are we to make plans to sin, to fulfill the lusts of the flesh, because a little sin defiles the whole body (Rom. 13:14; Gal. 5:9, 13; Ps. 19:12–14; Mic. 2:1).

If you live in the flesh, you shall die, but if you live in the Spirit, you put to death the deeds of the body and you shall live (Rom. 8:13). Therefore, allow God to order your steps and do not allow sin to rule you (Ps. 119:133). But some people seek their own and not the things that are of Jesus Christ (Phil. 2:21; 1 Tim. 6:9–10; James 3:13–16; John 5:41, 44; 1 Cor. 13:5).

You should be a new creature, where old things are passed away and all things are new, born again, spiritually (2 Cor. 5:16–17; 11:1–4; John 3:3–7; Rom. 8:5–14).

Born again, a new creature, not of the will of the flesh, blood, or mankind, but of the will of God (John 1:10–13), because flesh and blood cannot enter heaven (John 3:3–7; 1 Cor. 15:42–52; Gal. 5:16, 24–25; 1 Thess. 4:14–17).

God rules by his power, forever, and his eyes sees the nations. Let not rebellious people exalt themselves (Ps. 66:7).

There is no wisdom, understanding, or counsel against God nor has anyone taught him or counseled him (Prov. 21:30; Isa. 40:12–17, 28–31).

They who believe and are baptized shall be saved, but they who do not believe shall be damned (Mark 16:16; Rev. 20:10; 21:8, 27; 22:14–15; John 3:3–7; Acts 2:36–39; 8:14–17; 10:42–48; 19:1–6).

Angels in heaven rejoice when even one sinner repents, and after a person is born again of the water and of the Spirit, they are a new person. Old things are passed away and all things become new (Luke 15:1–10; John 3:3–7; 2 Cor. 5:17).

If a person is still alive, it is never too late to repent, to turn to Christ wholeheartedly, and to turn away from sins to live a new life on earth and eternally in heaven (Re. 21:8, 27; 22:14–15).

ABORTING INNOCENT BABIES IS CRUCIFYING BABIES

John the Baptist, as a fetus, jumped for joy in his mother's womb and uterus when Mary entered the room with Jesus in her womb (Luke 1:13–16, 39–44). But doctors who perform abortions cause helpless fetuses to jump, dodge, and try to avoid sharp destructive devices that purposely puncture the fetus until it dies. This practice has been seen in videos where the unborn baby runs for its life from the deadly sharp instrument. Speaking of the birth of Jesus, President Obama never included the name of Christ, Bible scripture, or anything from the Bible in his Christmas cards, because he was a version of the antichrist.

God formed Isaiah and Jeremiah while they were fetuses and called them to be his servants before they were even born (Isa. 49:1, 5; Jer. 1:5). Therefore, the life of a baby begins at conception (Ruth 4:13). And just as God causes and allows his servants to suffer for his name's sake sometimes, Jeremiah at one point wished that he had never been born, but he concluded that he could not resist serving the Lord no matter how many people persecuted him for telling the truth about God (Jer. 20:8–9, 17–18). God told Isaiah to cry aloud and spare not and tell his people about their sins and transgressions (Isa. 58:1–2). And John the Baptist in the New Testament cried aloud while preaching repentance and sanctification (Matt. 3:1–3; Mark 1:3–4; John 1:23). God promises that whatever we lose for doing the right thing, he will restore it a hundredfold on earth, but you will be persecuted by worldly and evil people, and then God will welcome you into heaven where there will be no more pain, suffering, crying, or death (Mark 10:28–31; Rev. 21:1–8; Job 1; 2:1–10; 13:15–16; 42; 1 Cor. 7:25–34; Luke 14:25–27, 33; 22:39–46).

The Apostle Paul was set aside to do God's work from the time he was in his mother's womb, although he was an anti-Christian and persecutor of the church as a younger man (Gal. 1:15). So if you are considering having an abortion or have birthed your child into the world and are concerned with them becoming a troublemaker or are already a troublemaking child, God has and still does save and use troubled people for his purpose and for his pleasure while simultaneously making the parents proud too (Acts 8:1–3; 9:1–6; 22:7–8, 19–20; 26:10–11, 14–15; 1 Cor. 15:9; Gal. 1:13–15; Phil. 3:6; 1 Tim. 1:13).

David said that his life was cast on God while he was in the womb and that God held him up while he was a fetus (Ps. 22:9–10; 71:6). So please, cast your child's life on God now. After all, God is making and forming the child inside of your womb and no scientist really knows how God develops unborn babies, but the Lord God Almighty will help and protect mothers and unborn babies (Eccles. 11:5; Ps. 139:13; Isa. 44:2, 24). The Bible says that God carries the unborn baby from the mother's womb (Isa. 46:3). On judgment day, fetuses shall be transformed and caught up just like fully developed humans and taken to heaven. In heaven, stillborn babies, aborted babies, and babies who died on earth as infants will live forever (Isa. 65:17–23). But the parents, doctors, nurses, and supporters of abortions will be in jeopardy of going to hell (Rev. 21:8, 27; 22:14–15). In the Old Testament, God loved fetuses so much that the law called for the execution of people who caused a woman to miscarry (Exod. 21:22–25).

Abortions are not new to the world. At one time, Jeremiah had such a hard time working for the Lord that he wished he had been aborted (Jer. 20:14–18). And Job wished that he had never been born (Job 3:1–12). Remember he was called to be and ended up being a great man of God. Job also was upright before God, feared God, and despised evil and sin (Job 1:1). Shouldn't we all try to be like Christ, Job, and other righteous men and women in the Bible? (Job 24:1–11, 29, 31)

God says that the firstborn child is the beginning of your strength (Gen. 49:3; Deut. 21:17; Ps. 105:36). The firstborn male born of a woman who has never had children before is holy unto the Lord (Exod. 13:2; Num. 3:13; Luke 2:23). So go ahead and give birth to your child. But to abort any unborn baby, especially your firstborn male, you would be killing a child that God considers to be holy and separated unto him (Exod. 13:2; Num. 3:13; Luke 2:23). God says that he will gently lead pregnant women (Isa. 40:11). After the child is born, God will provide (Matt. 6:25–34). God says that he knows people who have little strength but still have not denied his Word or his name, and that he sets before them an open door to heaven and an open door of opportunity on earth that no one can close, but he will say to hypocrites, "Depart from me, you worker of iniquity" (Matt. 7:21–23; Mic. 3:11; Luke 13:24–27).

There were people in the Bible who were barren and could not have children, and they prayed to God for the ability to conceive and birth children. But there are women nowadays who can conceive children, but they had abortions. Others used birth control for so long or used high health risk birth control to the point that they can no longer conceive a child, not to say that all forms of birth control are wrong.

It is a blessing to have children, especially considering that certain women in the Bible could not have children, because they were barren. Sarah was barren but ended up having Abraham, the father of all nations (Heb. 11:11). Rachel was barren but ended up having Judah, who started the tribe that Jesus came from (Gen. 29:31–35). Samson's mother was barren but birthed the physically strongest man to ever live (Judg. 13:1–

5, 24). Samuel's mother was barren but cried to the Lord for a child. She later gave birth to the author of 1 and 2 Samuel (1 Sam. 1:4–20). Elizabeth, John the Baptist's mother, was barren but gave birth to the greatest man to ever live, second to Jesus (Luke 1:5–7, 13; 7:24–26; Matt. 11:11). These women could not have kids but prayed to God for children. God answered their prayers, and their children ended up being some of the greatest people to ever live. Nowadays we have women who can have children but desire to kill them.

LATE-TERM ABORTIONS AND PARTIAL-BIRTH ABORTIONS ARE MURDERS

An abortion is the killing of a fetus or unborn baby. The Bible says, "Thou shalt not kill" (Exod. 20:13; Matt. 5:21–26). God is the only one who can kill or make alive (Deut. 32:39; 1 Sam. 2:6–7; 2 Kings 5:7; James 4:11–12).

Because we cannot make anyone live, we should not make anyone die. God says that if you can do as he does, then he will confess that you can also save yourself from hell (Job 40:1–14). All murderers, liars, nonbelievers, and whoremongers go to hell, unless they repent and stand against that sin (Rev. 21:8, 27; 22:14–15). Christ says, "Be not afraid of people who can kill the body, and after that can do no more to you. But I forewarn you whom you shall fear. Fear God, who after he has killed, also has power to cast you into hell, yes, I say unto you, fear him" (Luke 12:4–5).

Some people think that it is not murder to kill a fetus because they say it is not a human being yet, calling it "partial birth abortion," which is even more evil. But if a pregnant woman is murdered, the murderer would most likely be charged with two murders. The law of the land has become so evil nowadays, especially under the administration of Pres. Barack Obama who, along with the Supreme Court, took abortion rights to a higher and more evil level when they made it legal according to man's law to abort a baby that has been in the mother's womb for several months. The so-called morning after pill is not the same as abortion, because there truly is not a fetus or developed baby in the womb just one to two days after having sex. Remember, the "abortion pill" that some women used prior to the eighth or ninth week is murder and defiles the temple of God which is the human body (1 Cor. 3:16–23; 6:9–20; Eph. 2:19–22; Heb. 3:4–19; 4:1; Rom. 6:23).

Chris Christie former governor of New Jersey, said in April 2023 that the state of New Jersey allows babies to be aborted in the ninth month of pregnancy. He claimed to be pro – life, but he also said that he agreed with the law that allows unborn babies to be murdered in the ninth month of pregnancy. He sounded more like a hypocrite, a murderer, and a devil and not pro - life.

YOUR BODY BELONGS TO GOD, NOT TO YOU

A woman does not have the right to abort a child, and her body does not belong to her, but to God, and it is not her choice because the body of a human is the temple of God for him to dwell in (Luke 17:20–21; 1 Cor. 3:16–23; 6:9–20; Eph. 2:19–22; Heb. 3:4–19; 4:1; Rom. 6:23).

God does not dwell in temples made with hands, but in holy humans (Acts 7:48; 17:24). Jesus and Peter described their bodies as temples, and when we die, our earthly temple will be dissolved, but we will receive a building from God, a house not made with hands, for eternity (John 2:19–21; 2 Cor. 5:1; 2 Pet. 1:12–15).

If a woman kills a baby inside of her body, God will not dwell inside of that polluted, evil, and sinful body, unless she truly repents; but if not, the body of the woman could be destroyed by God, as she destroyed her child (1 Cor. 3:16–17; Heb. 3:6; Ps. 5:4; Rom. 6:23).

There is a time in the Bible when God killed the fetus and the mother when the mother lived in and embraced sin (Isa. 13:18). On judgment day, we shall see God like he is, and we shall be like him (Phil. 3:17–21; 1 John 3:2; Ps. 17:14–15).

But we cannot be like him in heaven if we do not strive to be like him on earth. The Bible says that we must live godly in this present world too (Titus 2:11–15). Remember, the Lord's Prayer says, "Let there be done on earth as it is in heaven" (Matt.

6:10). When we see God like he is, and when we become like him in heaven, he and we will not be gay; an abortionist or one who believes in abortions; a drunkard, drug dealer, drug addict, fornicator, thief, adulterer, child molester, idolater, or a participant in pornography; one who dresses in a sexually revealing way; anti-Christian; or lovers of money. For the love of money is the root to all evil and causes many hurtful sorrows (1 Cor. 6:9–11; 1 Tim. 6:6–12; 2 Kings 5:15–27).

Some money and certain riches are deceitful (Matt. 13:3–9, 18–23).

PARTAKERS AND SUPPORTERS OF ABORTIONS ARE ALSO PUNISHED BY GOD

The Bible says, "Be not partakers of other people's sins, that you may not receive the sickness and punishment that they receive for their sins. Keep yourself pure" (1 Tim. 5:22; Rev. 18:4). When Christ returns and we see him as he is, he will have children with him and all the babies that were killed in abortions (Luke 18:16). Christ says that out of the mouth of babes is his praise perfected (Matt. 21:15–16; Ps. 8:2). Jesus says that heaven consists of many children and that we must be as children as well to go to heaven (Matt. 18:1–6; 19:13–15).

Notice that the scripture says that if you harm a child, you may as well tie a weight around your neck and jump into the ocean, because that would be less painful than the punishment that God has for people who hurt and kill children and unborn children. Also, Christ says that kids have special angels who talk to God face to face (Matt. 18:10). Thus, medical personnel who perform abortions, the female who had the abortion, and all those who supported it would be better off tying a large stone around their neck and jump in the sea, unless they repent and turn away from their evil sins and live a life of sanctification (Matt. 18:1–6, 10; Heb. 2:11; 11:16; John 17:17–19; Isa. 29:23).

Evil happens to people who do not obey the Lord and who commit sins, such as adultery, fornication, murder, rebellion, voodoo, witchcraft, and blasphemy. God says that he will see whose words will stand, his or sinners (Jer. 44:15–29).

Whoever takes part in, allows, pays for, or agrees to an abortion is just as guilty as the one who the abortion is performed on and will be punished by God along with them (Job 8:20; 1 Tim. 5:22; Rev. 18:4; 2 Chron. 28:13).

A WOMAN'S RIGHT TO CHOOSE

In most states, people do not have the right to choose what they do with their bodies in terms of wearing or not wearing a seatbelt in an automobile because man's laws are designed to protect people from serious injury, and even death, if a wreck should happen. But women have a right to kill an unborn baby, even though they are not allowed to potentially kill themselves if an automobile wreck should happen. That is very hypocritical of lawmakers. When it comes to a woman's right to choose and what she does with her body, why isn't prostitution legal in all states and all countries? It is a matter of societies doing what is right in one sense and what is evil in another sense. According to some laws of the world, a woman cannot legally choose to do what she wants with her body in terms of prostitution, but she can choose to do what she wants with her body in terms of killing an unborn and helpless baby.

Speaking of prostitution, in the Bible, a woman once prostituted her body to conceive a baby, among other things (Gen. 38:12–30). If a woman should deceive a man nowadays, whether she is a prostitute or not, the man must not force her to have an abortion.

Speaking of choice, what if the father wanted his child and begged the woman not to abort the child? He should have input because the child belongs to him as well, but sinners and supporters of abortion will say in error that it is the woman's body, and she has the right to do what she pleases. However, if the child is allowed to be born, the law says that the father has the right to make decisions regarding the child. Some married women have abortions without telling their husbands. So, husbands, and all men, if a woman who believes in abortions is suddenly and mysteriously sick, or low on energy, or taking time off work, she may be recovering from having an abortion.

GUILT AFTER HAVING AN ABORTION

Research, confessions, and testimonies by many women reveal that some women who have aborted babies feel terrible and guilty and even have emotional and psychological problems in the future. Some no longer can become pregnant, whether it is punishment from God or self-inflicted stress caused by guilt, or some type of medical problem caused by doctors during the abortion.

WHEN IS THE WRONG TIME TO HAVE A CHILD

A woman told Christ, "Blessed is the womb that gave birth to him and the breasts that he sucked when he was a baby," but Christ told her, "Blessed are they who obey God" (Luke 11:27–28). Therefore, when you give birth to your unborn baby, your womb too is blessed, your body and soul are blessed, and you will be obeying God. Children are God's heritage, and the fruit of your womb is his reward and yours (Ps. 107:41; 127:3–5; 1 Chron. 4:27).

Children can be your help in old age and in sickness (Ruth 4:13–17). One may say that it is not a good time to have a child. There is no better time to have a child considering what Mary, the mother of Jesus, and Moses's mother went through. To try to prevent the birth of Jesus and Moses, the leaders of the nation killed the male babies (Matt. 2:13–16; Rev. 12:1–8; Exod. 1:15–22; 2:1–10).

That was not a good time to have a child, but they fought to have their child anyway. There were also other times in the Bible when the evil enemy killed infants and pregnant women (2 Kings 8:10–12; 15:16).

Notice in the scripture about Moses, how God blessed the nurses with new houses, among other things, who would not kill the children. That same scripture says that the nurses were lively, not deadly murderers. If you fear God, it will be well with you and your children (Deut. 5:29; Exod. 20:20; Prov. 23:17).

And do not worry about how you will take care of the baby, because God knows what his servants need, and he provides (Matt. 6:25–34; Luke 12:30–31). Even if your mother abandoned or neglected you, God says, "Can a mother forget and not have compassion on the child of her womb? She may forget, but I will never forget, says the Lord" (Isa. 49:15). We must walk in the fear of God and in the comfort of the Holy Ghost (Acts 9:31).

If Mary had an abortion, she and the whole world would go to hell. When women nowadays refused to abort their unborn child, the child will not grow up to be Jesus, but they may grow up to be gifted in some way and highly talented for the name of Jesus. And if our women nowadays cannot or will not remain virgins like Mary did, at least our women can refuse to kill unborn babies and fetuses. It is bad enough to lose your virginity, but it is evil and wicked to allow someone to enter your womb and kill fetuses and babies. And God hates and is angry with wicked people every day, until they truly repent (Ps. 5:4–7; 7:11; 11:5–7; 34:16; Isa. 5:20–25; 13:6–13). The Bible says to not know a wicked person nor to set a wicked thing before you (Ps. 101:3–4). Thus, the doctors who perform abortions are wicked. The Bible says that people who love the Lord hate evil (Ps. 97:10). The Lord is also jealous of sinners' commitment to their gods, idols, and sins (Exod. 20:5; 34:14; Deut. 4:24; 5:9; 6:15; 29:18–20; 32:16; Josh. 24:19; Dan. 5:23; 1 Kings 14:22; Ps. 79:5; Isa. 42:13; Ezek. 8:3–5; 16:38, 42; Zeph. 3:8; 1 Cor. 10:21–22)

MERCY AND FORGIVENESS FROM GOD

God is rich in mercy, he loves us, and by grace, we are saved (Eph. 2:2–5). God's mercies are new every morning but notice that those same merciful scriptures also speak of punishment from God and state that the Lord is good to people who wait for him, to the soul who seeks him, and that it is good for a person to both hope and quietly wait for the Lord (Lam. 3:15–26; Mic. 2:1; Ps. 19:12–14).

And that scripture about mercy also applies to the mercy that we all need just to wake up in the morning, because if it had not been for the death of Christ, we all would be dead. Jesus will return unexpectedly on judgment day like a thief in the night, but he also cuts off the life of people unexpectedly like a thief in the night (1 Thess. 5:1–11; 2 Pet. 3:10–18; Luke 12:13–21; Job 24:13–17).

Paul said that God had mercy on a man who was sick nearly to death while serving the Lord in righteousness, so again, if you wake up in the morning, God has already had mercy on you, especially if you are living in sin (Phil. 2:25–30). Lot procrastinated before he left Sodom and Gomorrah, and God had mercy on him, but Lot's wife looked back at the city while leaving and was turned into a pillar of salt. Notice how Lot warned his sons-in-law, but they did not take heed and died, but

God had mercy on Lot who lingered after knowing better and after warning others (Gen. 19:1–28). This happened the next morning after Lot warned them, so again, God's mercies are new every morning (Lam. 3:22–23; Ps. 92:1–2; Isa. 33:2).

But every morning someone falls short of his mercy and suffers pain and even death (Heb. 4:1; 1 Cor. 10:1–14; Deut. 28:58–59).

Just as God's mercy is new every morning, when we are in trouble, God's grace and strength is new every morning to people who ask of him and wait on him (Isa. 33:2).

On November 20, 2016, the media reported that the Catholic pope announced that the Catholic Church had started to allow women who had abortions to be forgiven by allowing them to confess to the priest. Before this time, women who had abortions were reportedly never forgiven, according to the Catholic Church. The Catholic Church is right when they say abortions are evil, but they are wrong when they say confession to a priest is required for forgiveness. Women who have had abortions are forgiven when they go before the throne of God through Jesus Christ, repent for their sins, never have another abortion, and stand against abortions because Christ is our High Priest (Heb. 4:14–16; John 5:20–27; 14:1, 6; 1 John 2:1; 2 John 1:9; Acts 4:12).

In 2018, the nation of Ireland voted to legalize abortion, sending a terrible defeat to the Catholic Church who is right for trying to uphold the ban of abortions. This too proves that most Catholic people are good people.

Abortions and other sins are forgiven by God when participants in sins have godly sorrow and not simply worldly sorrow and guilt. We must repent and show God that we have a contrite heart about our past sins (Isa. 57:15; 66:1–2; Ezra 9:6; 2 Cor. 7:9–10; Ps. 34:15–18; 38:15–18; 51:17; 85:8; Ezek. 18:21–22).

As stated earlier, we are children of God only when we obey

him and are holy, sanctified, and separate from the world, and abortion is wicked and worldly (Acts 5:32; Luke 11:13; John 14:13–18, 26–27; Phil. 2:15; 1 Pet. 1:13–17; Rom. 8:1, 5–17; 2 Cor. 6:17–18; Deut. 32:4–5; Matt. 12:46–50; Mark 3:31–35).

POSSIBLE PUNISHMENT AFTER FORGIVENESS

When Jesus told the woman who was caught in adultery that she was forgiven, he also told her—and other sinners who he ministered to—to sin no more or a worse thing will happen to you (John 5:14; 8:3-12). Some people ask why the Jews didn't attempt to kill the man who was caught in adultery with the woman, as the law permitted for adultery and for losing one's virginity (Lev. 20:10; Num. 5:27; Deut. 22:20-22; Ezek. 16:25-34).

Maybe he had already been stoned to death, maybe he had not been found or brought forward yet, or maybe he was not mentioned because neglectful men who translated the Bible into different languages failed to include what happened to the man.

We do know that David was a man who committed adultery with a married woman and God punished David by killing his newborn son and by allowing David's adult son to force him into exile or David would have been killed by his son who did temporarily take all of David's possessions, including the entire kingdom (2 Sam. 11; 12:1-24; 15; 1 Kings 14:8; 15:3-5).

Therefore, we must not look at David's evil sin and think that God forgave him without terrible consequences.

ABORTIONS ARE CRUCIFIXIONS AND CHILD SACRIFICES UNTO THE DEVIL

God is the God of the living and not of the dead, for all "live" unto him (Luke 20:38), including unborn babies and fetuses—they are "alive." That is why Christ rose from the dead. We are God's offspring, and it is because of him that we live, move, and have our being. We must seek God and not false gods, because even though it seemed like God was hard against idolatry in the Old Testament, he is even harder nowadays, and we must believe in the resurrection (Acts 17:21–34). When scripture says that God is the God of the living and not of the dead, it is referring to the resurrection of the saved (Rom. 14:7–9). He is not a dead God like other gods of the world. And God never required his people to sacrifice their children in death like some religions have (Jer. 7:31; Isa. 57:3–6; Gen. 22:1–13).

But when people have abortions, they sacrifice their unborn child to the devil, because the devil is of death (Deut. 18:10; Lev. 18:21; 20:2–5; Ezek. 16:20–21).

Although God did sacrifice his only begotten Son, after we learn the truth, there is no sacrifice for willful sin because you would have planned to sin and followed through with your sinful and evil plans, and it is a fearful thing to fall into the hands of the "living" God (Heb. 10:26–31; Exod. 20:18–19; Deut. 5:23–26; Rom. 1:18–32; 2 Thess. 2:10–15).

Therefore, not all sins are the same, as excuse makers say. They are all the same when we truly repent, ask for forgiveness, and stand against those sins but they are different in terms of how we are punished by God for certain sins. When heterosexuals have sex before marriage, it is sin. God created sex for a man and a woman in a marriage. God did not create homosexual sex. The devil created homosexual sex. Therefore, fornication and adultery between a man and a woman is wrong because God's rule was broken in how sex that he created should be performed, but God never created homosexual sex. Homosexual sex was created by demons and the devil.

Jesus says that some pregnant women and nursing women in certain parts of the world will have a hard time during the last days while people are being punished for their sins and evil works (Matt. 24:17–22; Luke 21:20–24). But if a woman aborts a child to simplify her life, she will suffer even more tribulation during those very same days of world tribulation, because sins like abortions are some reasons that these last days are so hard.

GOVERNMENT FINANCED ABORTIONS

The administration of Pres. Barack Obama told a prolife organization that if they protest abortion clinics, they will not receive tax exemptions. Pres. Barack Obama was not the first president of the United States to support abortions, but he worked hard to legalize the financing of abortions by insurance companies and with Medicaid, which means taxpayers who do not believe in abortions would be helping to pay for killing unborn babies. President Obama also worked hard to allow teenaged girls to have abortions without the parent's knowledge. Some states made it legal to kill well-developed babies who have been in their mother's stomach for several months. But if the first fruits are holy and sanctified, the whole body is holy (Rom. 11:16–25; Rev. 2:1–5). These fruits can be the baby in the woman's stomach and the woman herself for not killing her child.

Abortions are also used by the government to control the population. They allow chemicals in food and in herbicides and pesticides to control how many people die each year, and they allow abortions to control how many are born each year. Then came the Mexican migration into the United States, which was not a bad thing. Mexicans were allowed to enter because Americans needed them in the labor force, but the population increased by millions. So the government relied on abortions even more to help control the population. A curse from God has devoured the earth because many people are defiled, and many of earth's inhabitants choose to be desolate (Isa. 24:4–6).

People accept and support unrighteous politicians instead of God's Word because the politicians will make life better in one sense. When a nation suffers financially, economically, or in any other way, that is nothing compared to facing God's wrath of disasters and tragedies sent from heaven, not to mention hell as the ultimate punishment. God says, "Shall I not visit for these things... Shall not my soul be avenged on such a nation" (Jer. 5:9, 29; 14:10; 2 Sam. 21:1; 2 Kings 21:10–16; Luke 13:1–5; Neh. 9:33–35).

People who supported Obama and other politicians because those politicians allowed them to receive assistance or benefits may be forgetting that God says that he himself provides us with daily benefits (Ps. 68:19; 103:2; 106:5; 116:12).

There is no need to support anti-God politicians when we trust in and serve the Lord with all our heart, mind, soul, and strength (Mark 12:30; Luke 10:27; Deut. 6:5; Prov. 30:5).

It is better to trust in the Lord than to put confidence in politicians and other humans because the Lord is on your side and humans cannot cause us to fall when God is on our side (Ps. 56:4; 118:6–9). When we trust in the Lord with all our heart and lean not on our own understanding, when we are not self-righteous, when we fear the Lord, and when we acknowledge him in all our ways, God says that he provides health and strength for our bodies and fills our homes with necessities. Then we must honor the Lord with our possessions and the first fruits of our increase (Prov. 3:5–10). Ungodly and anti-Christian politicians should be like Josiah and Hezekiah who were the second and third best kings in the Bible, King Jesus being the first best. They served the Lord in holiness and sanctification and obeyed his Word, and God protected them and caused them to prosper (2 Kings 18:1, 5–7; 23:19–25). We must do as Moses did when he was a politician who refused to enjoy the pleasures of sin for a season (Heb. 11:23–27).

ABORTION IS AN EVIL INVENTION CREATED BY HUMANS

God does not help evildoers (Job 8:20). As stated before, God made mankind upright, but they have sought out many wicked inventions (Eccles. 7:26–29; Ps. 33:13–15). In the Old Testament, the Bible says, "You answered them, O Lord God, you were a God who forgave them, though you punished them for their inventions" (Ps. 99:8). In the New Testament, God says that people who participate with evil inventions are worthy of death (Rom. 1:21–32). And they will die if they do not repent and live a righteous life, because the consequences and wages of sin is death (Rom. 6:23; Ezek. 7:13; 18:4). During the use of those inventions, God punishes us, but he is ready to forgive if we repent and turn away from the evil practices of those inventions (Ps. 106:29, 39–48; Eccles. 7:26–29; Ps. 33:13–15).

Notice in those same scriptures how hard it was for God to find a righteous woman. These inventions provoke God to anger, and in return, disease and other problems are in the land (Ps. 106:29). Abortions are the works of humans, which defile you (1 Cor. 3:16–23; 6:9–20). Those who partake in abortions are whoring after mankind's inventions (Ps. 106:29, 39–48). Anything not done by faith in Christ is sin (Rom. 14:23). The just shall live by faith, and it is impossible to please God without faith (Rom. 1:16–18; Hab. 2:4; Gal. 3:11; Heb. 6:1–6; 10:38; 11:1, 6).

For we walk by faith, not by sight (2 Cor. 5:7). The person that is lifted up like God and kills like God is not right (Hab. 2:4). You are justified by faith (Rom. 5:1), and faith does not tell you to kill an unborn baby. If you repent, God will forgive you, but if you do not repent and stand against abortions, you may not live to see the future (Rom. 1:28–32). When God forgives you, he may still punish you in some measure or degree for using such an evil invention (Ps. 99:8).

FORNICATION AND ADULTERY CAUSES UNWANTED PREGNANCIES

The Holy Bible scripture says, "Flee fornication, because your body was not made for that" (1 Cor. 6:18–20). If necessary, run from fornication, like Joseph did in the Old Testament when the king's wife tried to seduce him (Gen. 39). And in the New Testament, another man named Joseph did not have sex with Mary the mother of Jesus while being engaged to marry her (Matt. 1:18–21; Luke 1:27). Elijah lived with a widow for a while during a great drought and famine, but they did not have sex (1 Kings 17:1, 8–24). Maybe the widow tried to sexually seduce Elijah, and he resisted like Joseph did when he fled from the presence of the king's wife, or maybe she did not try to seduce him. But we do know that Elijah did not try to seduce her and that no sexual activity occurred, because there are only four people who have already made it to heaven, and they are the ones who came down from heaven in the first place (John 3:13). That is Jesus, Enoch, Elijah, and Melchisedec (Acts 1:9; Gen. 5:11; Heb. 7:1–3; 11:5; Gen. 5:22–24; 2 Kings 2:1–14).

Obviously, a person of that spiritual caliber would not have sinned against the Lord in that manner.

Job said that he would not even look at a woman other than

his wife (Job 1:1, 7–12; 31:1–12). The Apostle Paul said that it is good for a man to not touch a woman, to avoid fornication, and that let every man have his own wife and every woman her own husband (1 Cor. 7:1–2; Col. 3:18–21; 1 Pet. 3:1–12; Deut. 5:21; Titus 2:1–8; Eph. 5:22–33).

We must not desire our neighbor's wife or husband (Deut. 5:21; Jer. 5:7–8; 29:23; Ezek. 18:5–18; 22:10–14).

Some people speak peace to their neighbor and have evil intentions in their heart at the same time (Ps. 28:3–5). But the Bible tells us to build our neighbors up in the Lord (Rom. 15:2). A neighbor includes more than the person next door, but in God's sight, neighbors are all people (Luke 10:27–37). And if people did not participate in fornication and adultery, they would not have unwanted pregnancies.

ABORTING BABIES OF INCEST & RAPE OR TO SAVE THE LIFE OF THE MOTHER

When it comes to aborting an early pregnancy to save the life of the mother, that may be the only time that the decision to abort falls into the hands of humans without being totally against God. In this case, doctors would be taking the life of an embryo or fetus who may not live anyway, to save the life of a mother who has lived and can continue to live. But a late term or fully developed baby should, if possible, not be aborted or killed, especially if a cesarean section, also called a C – section, can save the life of both the mother and the baby. Aborting babies to save the life of the mother must also have strict guidelines that prevent "pro – choice" and "pro – abortion" doctors from acting too swiftly and making hasty and quick decisions to abort while knowing that the mother's life was not truly in jeopardy. To abort an early pregnancy to save the life of the mother is a life or death decision, but to abort a pregnancy for all other reasons is selfishness and a death and death decision, which would be the death of the baby and the spiritual death of the mother, making herself the walking dead (Matt. 22:32; 1 Tim. 5:6; Eccles. 7:15; Matt. 8:19–22; 23:27; Rev. 3:1–3, 17–22; Jude 1:12; James 2:20).

Remember, the Spirit of God is against the flesh, and the flesh is against the Spirit of God, in reference to fleshly and worldly decisions (Gal. 5:16–26; 1 Pet. 2:11–12).

Also remember that the world loves its own evil people, and a friend of the world is an enemy of God (James 4:2–4; John 1:10–12; 15:18–19; 1 John 2:15–17; 3:13; Rom. 6; 8:1–16; Gal. 5:16–26; 1 Pet. 2:11; 1 Cor. 1:10; 2:9–16; Rom. 15:5–6; Phil. 3:16–21).

Regarding rape and incest, if the rape or incest is addressed within a few days the "morning after pill" can prevent the pregnancy before an embryo or fetus is even developed. Keep in mind that God is the only one who can kill and make alive, save, and destroy, but preventing a pregnancy before it begins is not aborting, killing, or murdering a baby (James 4:12; Deut. 32:39; 1 Sam. 2:6–7; 2 Kings 5:7).

If the female waits too long to take the "morning after pill" after being raped or victimized in incest, they should still give birth to the child and put him or her up for adoption if they feel that they cannot raise the child. The so called "abortion pill" is a chemical – based pill that some women used to kill their baby when they were less than eight or nine weeks pregnant, which is also murder. The chemicals in the pill are also dangerous to the woman's body and defiles the body which is the temple of God (1 Cor. 3:16–23; 6:9–20; Eph. 2:19–22; Heb. 3:4–19; 4:1; Rom. 6:23).

The mother may say that if she gave birth to a child that resulted from rape, there will be someone walking around with their blood in them and the blood of a rapist. If the mother kills the baby, sure she will get rid of the blood of the rapist, but she would also kill her own blood and have sinful blood on her hands, making her a murderer and worse than a rapist. The same thing applies to incest cases and in the case of a very young girl becoming pregnant. It is a tough situation, but "thou shalt not kill" means just what it says (Matt. 5:21–26). This is the love of God—that we keep his commandments, and his commandments are not grievous (1 John 5:3). For thousands of years before abortions became common practice and popular, victims of incest and rape, and young girls who became pregnant had to give birth to their child. There were evil practices in ancient Athens in Europe when unwanted babies were left on a hillside to die, and that too was not against the law, but it was extremely evil, just as abortions are extremely evil.

God can cause a baby conceived in rape and incest to be a blessing as well, as he has done before in the past. People who have abortions and people who have willful sex without being married are saying they will not walk in God's ways to find rest for their souls (Jer. 6:16). Christ says, "Come to me, all you who labor, and are heavy laden, and I will give you rest. Take my yoke upon you and learn of me, for I am meek, gentle, and lowly in heart, and you will find rest for your souls. For my yoke is easy and my burden is light" (Matt. 11:28–30).

THE HEARTS, THOUGHTS, AND ACTIONS OF ABORTIONISTS

God says regarding the enemies of his people, "Many people have gathered against you... But they do not know the thoughts of the Lord, nor do they understand his counsel, for he shall destroy them" (Mic. 4:5; John 8:31–47; Judg. 11:23–24).

That was in the Old Testament and before Christ died and rose from the dead. But nowadays, God is requiring all people everywhere to repent or face a strong possibility of dying sooner than later and going to hell (Luke 24:46–49; Acts 14:8–18; 17:26, 29–31).

The wicked, through pride, will not seek God, because God is not in their thoughts (Ps. 10:4). The anger of the Lord shall not return until he has executed and until he has performed the thoughts of his heart. In the latter days, they will consider it perfectly (Jer. 23:20). The Lord says, "I have spread out my hands all day unto a rebellious people, who walk in a way that is not good, after their own thoughts" (Isa. 65:2). God says, "I was grieved with that generation, and said, they do always err in their heart; and they have not known my ways. So, I swear in my wrath, they shall not enter my rest. Take heed, lest there be in any of you an evil heart of unbelief, in departing from the living God" (Heb. 3:7–12). God is God of the living and not of the dead, but abortionist and people who believe in, participate in, support, or perform abortions are people of the dead, not only because they believe in killing innocent babies but also because they are the walking dead themselves (Matt. 22:32; 1 Tim. 5:6; Eccles. 7:15; Matt. 8:19–22; 23:27; Rev. 3:1–3, 17–22; Jude 1:12; James 2:20).

Everyone should say to God, "Search me, O God, and know my heart. Try me, and know my thoughts, and see if there be any wicked way in me and lead me in the way everlasting" (Ps. 139:23–24). Hallelujah!

GOD IS LIFE BUT HE PUNISHES MURDERERS TERRIBLY

Christ came so that we shall have life and have it more abundantly, but the thief who is the devil and hypocrites who do evil things, including abortionist and participants in abortions, come to steal, to kill, and to destroy (John 10:10). Christ says that anyone who truly believes in him shall have rivers of living water flowing from their belly (John 7:38). The living water can be joy, happiness, prosperity, wealth, good health, peace, or long life, but the living water that flows from a woman's belly can also be her unborn baby. When we get to heaven, Christ promises fountains of living waters with no more tears, but participants in abortions are in jeopardy of not inheriting heaven (Rev. 7:13-17). God is God of the living and not of the dead (Luke 20:38). The grave cannot praise God, and this pertains to unborn babies who were killed, and to participants of abortion when God takes their life for killing unborn babies (Isa. 38:16–20; Ps. 6:5; 63:3-4; 88:10–12; 115:17; 116:9).

It is a fearful thing to be punished by the living God (Heb.10:22-31; Mic. 2:1; Ps. 19:12–14).

Vengeance belongs to God, and he will repay (Rom. 12:19–21; Nah. 1:1-3; 2 Thess. 1:7-9; Ps. 94; 1 Sam. 25:2-3, 39; Deut. 2;

25:17–19; 32:35–43).

The price we pay for sinning is death, especially when people are guilty of murder (Rom. 1:18–32; 6:23; 2 Thess. 2:10–15; 8:13–14; 1 Kings 13:11–24; 1 Cor. 11:23–30; Ezek. 7:13; 18:4; 33:11, 19–20; Deut. 30:19–20; Job 20:11; 24:19; 36:5–13; Ps. 1:5–6; Prov. 19:5, 9; 21:16; 27:20; 30:15–16; Isa. 5:14; 13:9; Josh. 7:1–13; 1 Chron. 10:13–14; Rev. 2:23; Matt. 18:11–14; Lam. 3:31–33; 1 Tim. 2:4; 2 Pet. 3:9; Luke 13:1–5).

COVID – 19 (CORONAVIRUS)

In March of 2020, there was a global outbreak of Coronavirus (also called COVID-19). This may have happened because of the world, including some Christians accepting; embracing; and supporting homosexuality, abortions, and late-term abortions. We do know that those abominations, murders, and evil, wicked sins were legalized on a global scale; and only a few years later, there was a global outbreak of Coronavirus, which was something the world had never seen or heard of before, just as global, and worldwide acceptance of anti-God practices were legalized globally like never before.

We do know that God promises to not allow disease, affliction, and adversity in our lands when we obey his Word; and that if we do not obey his Word, God says he allows prolonged disease and sickness in the land and even new diseases and illnesses that are not written in the Bible (Exod. 15:26; Deut. 7:12–15; 28:58–61; Rev. 2:18–29; Rom. 5:9; Jer. 30:12–15; Ps. 38; 107:17).

Most pandemics and natural disasters are a result of God being displeased with our sinful actions. Many people live by laws and practices that they made or supported; and that results in pain, natural disasters, bad weather, sorrow, sickness, disease, death, and destruction (2 Kings 17:19; Ps. 28:4–5).

Most people did not acquire the Coronavirus. God is too gracious and merciful to allow that to happen. But he does have a way of getting everyone's attention, instilling fear in everyone, and causing almost everyone to pray unto him, but some people are too hardhearted to pray. God punishes people harder who do not take heed to his rebuke and warnings and who do not choose the fear of the Lord (Prov. 1:28–30). The Lord will take sickness out of the land when people turn again to him, confess his name in righteousness, pray, repent and turn away from their rebellion (Exod. 23:25; Deut. 7:15; 28; 29:2–6; 2 Chron. 7:14; Matt. 13:14–15; Luke 19:37–42; Isa. 6:8–10; Lev. 20:6–27; Jer. 4:22).

We should not be surprised when we see and hear of new diseases, destruction, and death because the Bible says that in these last days, dangerous and perilous times will continue to happen due to sin, hypocrisy, blasphemy, and rebellion and that our generation will experience more tribulation and trouble than the world has ever known or will ever hear of again. Because most people do not accept the love of the truth of God's Word (Matt. 24:21; Mar. 13:19; Dan. 12:1; 2 Thess. 2; 1 Tim. 4:1–3; Mic. 5:2, 4, 15).

The last days for most of us are the days before we die because most people will not live to see the last day of the earth's existence (2 Tim. 3:1–7; 1 John 2:18). But God allows most of us to die sooner or later because most of us must die to get to heaven unless we are alive on the last day of the earth's existence. Saved people who are alive on the last day of the earth's existence will be instantly transformed into angels without ever dying (1 Thess. 4:13–18; 1 John 2:18).

Not everyone who died from COVID-19 is going to hell and not everyone who died from COVID-19 was an enemy of God. But people who support worldly anti-God laws, practices, and policies are enemies of God (James 4:4; John 1:10–12; 15:18–19; 1 John 2:15–17; 3:13; Phil. 3:16–21).

If anyone thinks that COVID-19 had nothing to do with mankind legalizing homosexual marriages and abortions, including late term abortions, then do they think that God will never punish the world for that level of rebellion, blasphemy, and hypocrisy? God says, "Shall I not visit the earth for these sins?" (Prov. 19:23; Jer. 5:9, 29; 14:10). Sin separates us from our God (Isa. 1:15; 59:1–2; 64:4–8; Ps. 107:17–22; Mal. 2:2).

Some humans try to void God's Word, and that causes God to have a controversy with the inhabitants of the land and causes humans to not be able to go to work so God can work (Ps. 119:126; Job 37:7; Hos. 4:1–2). And if COVID-19 is not one of God's ways of punishing the world for embracing abortions and homosexuality, that only means that harder times are coming because God shall act regarding abortions and homosexuality. And Christ says that the tribulations, troubles, and diseases that we suffer are only the beginning of sorrows (Matt. 24:3–8). Some of those sorrows have come to past already during times like World War I and World War II, but the Bible says that times will be harder, and that trouble in our generations are only the beginning of sorrows (Matt. 24:3–8). God's Word will never return to him void. God eventually does exactly what he says he will do, whether he promises to send blessings or death and destruction (Isa. 14:24; 46:9–10; 55:10–11; Jer. 23:20; Ezek. 5:13; 6:9–10; 12:21–28; 22:14; 24:13–14; Dan. 9:12–14; Matt. 24:32–44; 2 Pet. 3:6–14; 2 Kings10:10).

Several scientists in April 2020 said that COVID-19 was not man-made, but that it did probably originate in China. Most people know that China was and maybe still is an extremely anti-Christ nation. Therefore, God may have used COVID-19 to punish them although some people believe that China created the virus to decrease their extremely large human population. Hopefully, it was not made by humans on purpose with evil intentions, but if it was made by humans, the Bible says that God made everything, even wicked people, for the day of evil (Prov. 16:2–7; Isa. 45:5–7; Lam. 3:37–40).

In other words, God sometimes uses evil inventions to punish people because the inventions are accessible to him, even if he did not create them himself. Those same scriptures also say that people who invent wicked things shall not go unpunished, and by the fear of the Lord, people depart from evil and that when a person's ways and works please the Lord, God makes even their enemies to be at peace with them (Prov.16:2–7).

The government of New York boldly embraced almost every anti-God law and practice that mankind created, and that is one reason they suffered so much. Louisiana also had a high number of COVID-19 cases, and they suffer a lot in Louisiana from hurricanes, floods, and other forms of adversity because Louisiana is basically the modern-day magic, sorcery, voodoo, and witchcraft capital of the United States. Mardi Gras crowds are believed to be the reason that COVID-19 cases were so high in Louisiana, but Mardi Gras itself is anti-Christian. Mardi Gras originated with pagan and heathen ties and is a time when people make one last effort to indulge in eating, drinking, and sinning before the celebration of the life, crucifixion, death, and resurrection of our Lord and Savior Jesus Christ. Mardi Gras ends on Fat Tuesday, and people have historically repented for their sins the following day on Ash Wednesday, which is the first day of Lent and the beginning of the preparation for Holy Week, Passion Week, Passover week, resurrection week, and Resurrection Day, erroneously called Easter by most people.

The harder people speak and stand against God, the harder his punishment is toward those people (Ps. 90:11; Jude 1:14– 25). Therefore, it is no coincidence that American and European nations suffered the most from COVID-19. It is one thing to be a non-Christian, but it is a lot worse to be a hypocrite, Christian. At least non-Christians in their nations do not pretend to be Christians, and God says that many so-called Christians are worse than people who do not claim to be Christians (Jer. 2:32–33; 5:28–31; 2 Chron. 33:9; Matt. 5:19; 23:15; 2 Kings 21:10–12; Lam. 4:6; Ezek. 16:47– 48; 1 Tim. 5:8; 1 Cor. 5:1).

God says that he will heal the land if people who are called by his name shall pray, repent, and turn from their wicked ways (2 Chron. 7:13 – 14; Isa. 6:8–10; Ezek. 33:31; Matt. 13:14–15; Luke 19:37–42; Deut. 29:2–6).

Killing unborn babies and supporting that practice is evil and wicked.

Remember, just as our leaders can cause great peace and prosperity in the land, our leaders can also cause God's wrath to strike the land. Just as was the case when the land suffered a great famine during the days of King David. David prayed to God, and God told David that the famine was punishment for the sins of King Saul, who was David's predecessor (2 Sam. 21:1). And it is highly likely that COVID-19 happened because of the wicked abortion and homosexual laws that President Barack Obama and other world leaders legalized.

REFERENCES

The Holy Ghost

The Holy Bible

ABOUT THE AUTHOR

Elijah Paul

Elijah Paul has published six books and is a Christian minister who has been in the ministry since the 1990's. All the author's initial developments of his books began by the direction of God Almighty as part of a much larger book nearly twenty-three years before he published his first book. The Lord showed the author the original vision that caused him to begin writing, and God gave additional visions through the years as the Lord revealed them to the author. The original work was written over a twenty-two-year period and consists of more than 1,400 pages and more than 2,000 topics. The author's original vision from God included a vision of a number 2, which caused the author to assume that the larger book would be published after two years of writing. As years passed, the author became worried that he was not fulfilling God's work and that pursuing advanced college degrees and handling adversities, afflictions, trials, and tribulations were delaying the larger book's completion date. As more years passed, the author assumed that the number 2 that he saw in the vision must have involved the number 12 which is a significant number in the Bible, but after the larger book was still far from being completed after twelve years, the author assumed that the vision of the number 2 must have been twenty years. And after twenty years of writing, the author felt that he had failed to fulfill God's calling and purpose. But when the larger book was finally finished after twenty-two years of writing, the author realized that the number 2 that he saw in the vision was twenty-two years and the year 2020. After twenty-two years of writing, God finally revealed to the author that the larger book will never be published as one huge book, but that several smaller books will be published from the original larger book. The first smaller book was taken out of the larger book and published in the year 2020. Therefore, the fulfillment of the vision of the number 2 is twenty-two years to finish writing, and the first book was published in the year 2020. The author plans to spend the rest of his life publishing books from his twenty-two years of documenting revelations from the Messiah.

BOOKS BY THIS AUTHOR

Slaveholders, Churches & Colonists Changed The Bible, The Greatest Identity Theft In Histroy. Black Jews & Black Egyptians Changed To White

One Lord, One Faith, One Baptism, All Questions Answered With Scriptures

God Is With You In Hard Times When You Think That He Is Not

Favor Of God, Forgetting Your Past, Remembering Where God Brought You From

BACK COVER SUMMARY

God commands us to be living sacrifices, and it is not God's desire that anyone should die. Christ died for all people, the Just for the unjust. Therefore, we should try to sacrifice and crucify as many sins out of our lives as possible. When we disobey the Word of God, we spiritually but not physically crucify Christ, because the Word is Christ. All presidents, kings, and queens have done some good things and some not-so-good things. This book focuses on President Obama who had a good upbringing as a child in a Muslim household, but Islam did not cause him to do things contrary to the Word of God. Most Founding Fathers and early presidents of the USA were not Christians or Muslims, but they sometimes crucified Christ. Presidents crucified Christ when they supported the system of women not being allowed to vote, and supported slavery, sharecropping, and oppression, and started certain wars. Some presidents allowed lynchings, which were a form of crucifixions. We often associate Christ's crucifixion only to his way of dying, but crucifixion was a method of the death penalty that the Romans used more than 2000 years ago on many people. Like the electric chair, gas chamber, lethal injection, firing squad, and lynching were methods of execution in recent history. Most people who were lynched where hanged as innocent people and without a court trial, causing Christ's Word to be crucified. The antichrist is not simply one person, but the Bible says many political antichrists have already come. The main point here is that God wants us to live and not die, and that if we crucify anything, crucify sin and not the Word of God. Be a living sacrifice, holy and acceptable to God, which is your reasonable service. While studying this book, readers will gain the wisdom to live a happy, prosperous and protected life with Christ as the head and forefront of your life.

www.ingramcontent.com/pod-product-compliance
Lightning Source LLC
Chambersburg PA
CBHW070641160426